A TO Z OF HAPPINESS AND SUCCESS

DR.C.K. KANTIYA

Become Shakespeare .com

First published in 2021 by
BecomeShakespeare.com

One Point Six Technologies Pvt Ltd,
123, Building J2, Shram Seva Premises,
Wadala Truck Terminus,
Wadala (E), Mumbai - 400037
T:+91 8080226699

ISBN: 978-93-90543-20-5

DEDICATED

TO ALL THE CHILDREN WITH SPECIAL NEEDS

I WANT YOU TO BELIEVE DEEP IN YOUR HEART THAT YOU ARE CAPABLE OF ACHIEVING ANYTHING YOU PUT YOUR MIND TO

*that you will *

NEVER LOSE

YOU EITHER WIN OR LEARN

Just go forth and aim for the skies

Universe has a lot to offer in the form of Happiness and Success.

FOREWORD

The A TO Z OF HAPPINESS AND SUCCESS is an insightful and excellent work of literature by Dr. C. K. Kantiya. It lets the readers delve deep into the nuances of life and how by being aware about ourselves we can be more happy and successful. Author has taken a very commendable decision of sharing his knowledge and experience in the form of this self-help, life changing motivational book. This book is an exemplary portrayal of human behavior and psychology, expressed in simple language, making it all the more relatable. There are 121 Articles in this book and every article is independent of other, all of them when put together are beautiful flowers of a life making garland of thoughts. It all comes down to treading our own paths to happiness and on the way evolving, exploring and being enchanted by the mysteries of life. I am confident that this book will be of great guidance to all readers at various stages of life. There are many people in this world who feel defeated before getting defeated and who infect deserve to win; this book will act as a panacea for all of them. This book may be used as a success guide by everyone who wishes to attain greater heights of success along with a sense of happiness. My best wishes and blessings to the author and I Salute his noble initiative of utilizing revenue of this book for supporting children with special needs.

ARVIND BHATT
(Motivational Trainer, Life Coach and Theatre Artist)

AUTHOR’S S PROFILE

Dr CHIRANJIV KUMAR KANTIYA is a registered Psychologist from Rehabilitation Council of India, a Trainer by profession and RJ by passion. He has diversified work experience of 19 years in Sales, Training, Marketing, Administration, Software development, Event Management, Media, and Academics.

He is certified approved FM RJ AIR and certified National Trainer of JCI India. “**CHIRANJIV**” is a sports person, Marathon Runner, NCC Cadet, Computer Science Graduate, (Management, Psychology and Computer Science Post graduate) with a **PhD** in Applied Psychology. He has presented National and International Research papers in the field of Psychology and Education, written articles for Newspapers and Psychology Magazines. He has been actively involved in various social activities and has a clear vision to work with Children with Special needs. He has excellent Oratory skills with extensive training experience in Academics and Corporate Industry.

CONNECT AUTHOR

Mail: atozofhappiness@gmail.com

FB: A TO Z OF HAPPINESS AND SUCCESS

YOU TUBE: A TO Z OF HAPPINESS AND SUCCESS

INTRODUCTION

THE QUEST OF TWO GERMANEVARIABLES which would make LIFE of Quality and Purpose, not only for me but for everyone ended up with HAPPINESS AND SUCCCESS.

You will be glad to know that complete life of an individual pivots rounds them only. The fact which struck me with wonder was that they are proportional to each other to a certain extent. In other words, if you are *Happy,* the chances are more that you will be successful in life. And in reverse, if you are successful, happiness will reside nearby. To spread the Happiness and Success mantras to entire humanity I have written this self-help book. This is a very simple book to read and understand as I have shortlisted words which are important both for Happiness and Success.

I am sure that we all remember the very first step of our English learning which started from A to Z. Keeping simplicity as mode of effective implementation and greater benefit, the book has been written in similar A to Z format. I am quite certain that this book is going to alter your perception towards life and people. You will start to keep a work life balance, cherish what you have, enjoy better relationship and be happier and successful. This book is purely based on my life experiences and the results may differ from person to person.

"Success is not the key to happiness; Happiness is the key to success.

If you love what you are doing, you will be successful."

- Albert Schweitzer.

CONTENTS

CHAPTER 1

A OF HAPPINESS AND SUCCESS

ACCEPTANCE

"Happiness can exist only in Acceptance."
-George Orwell.

"I was willing to accept what I couldn't change."
-APJ Abdul Kalam.

If I make this puissant statement simple by accepting the things the way they are, I am confident that you will be very elated as happiness is directly linked to your acceptance. Acceptance is looking at the face value of things and aligning with reality. In this world there are different religions, languages, beliefs, geographies, priorities, and choices. So, from today onwards, accept others as they are, even if you do not understand initially. If everything is alike in this world, life will become humdrum. Cherish the diversity and appreciate the differences for greater excitement, fun, happiness, and success.

Acceptance is the first step on the ladder of success. Life becomes simple when we start accepting people in their original form; most of us try to change others but the moment we realize that it is very easy to change ourselves, then our equation of life become easy and happiness starts multiplying. Though I am an

IT Graduate and Post Graduate, it was very difficult for me to do programming. Initially I struggled a lot and finally I accepted that I am not adept at programming and was candid enough to accept that I will not be enjoying a career in IT industry wherein we need to sit for long hours finding errors of others' programming. I accepted my drawbacks and started finding my strengths and realized that I am a gregarious man. I started looking for a job wherein my strength of speech and voice can be used. Finally, I managed to clear the auditions of AIR and started off as a Radio Jockey. This break helped me to get into corporate training industry. Accepting my original strength and weakness, I changed my industry from one that was highly lucrative to one which attracted my skills. I started enjoying my work and acquired qualifications complementing to my interest in psychology and people skills. Accepting your limitations and identifying strengths open new pathways of success. If you are short, accept it because you may see that some of the world class cricketers are not very tall. *As Stated by Carl Jung "We cannot change anything unless we accept it."*

Real growth happens when you accept your own originality, face the world with your strengths and work without holding any preconceived notions.

To live the life that you have dreamt of, start accepting people, places and situations and increase your acceptance in your surroundings for healthy relationships, happiness, and lots of success.

✣ ✣ ✣

APPRECIATION

"Be thankful for what you have; you will end up having more. If you concentrate on what you don't have, you will never, ever have enough."

-Oprah Winfrey.

"Happiness is found in the absence of expectation and a continuous focus on appreciation."

-Tony Robbins.

Appreciation is so entrancing that people naturally get attracted to you, the moment you appreciate them. It not only attracts people but also lots of positive vibes and is the key to our inner peace. We should appreciate what we have, our parents, teachers, brothers, sisters, neighbors, achievements, job, climate, and everything we have. Never let these precious moments go without being noticed and appreciated. Appreciation needs to be a daily activity. When we practice appreciation, joy will follow and happiness will multiply. To practice appreciation, we must first appreciate self then our friends and enemies too. This will make us feel important and valuable.

Let me share with you an example: While having dinner, do appreciate your mother, tell her that the food is very delicious and then glance at her face; all her fatigue goes away with a smile. Do appreciate at least 3 people daily: One yourself, second the person you love the most and third anyone you interact or come across for a genuine reason. Appreciate your strengths and weakness also, that will increase our awareness and gradually our mind find ways of making our weakness as strengths. Appreciate your defeats and failures also that will make you a better and strong person. **Mahatma Gandhi once said, "There is more to life than increasing its speed."** So, stop running so fast. Slow down a little bit, learn how to breathe, feel your pulse, your heart beat, feel the life and the energy that runs through and appreciate the life you now have. Appreciation improves quality of relationships both at home and at work place and you will attract more opportunities to perform and become successful.

***Appreciation is a habit which needs to be cultivated and should be a daily activity.* When this habit becomes part of our persona, we truly become positive individuals, looking for good in every person and situation.**

ATTITUDE

"It is very important to generate a good attitude, a good heart, as much as possible. From this, happiness in both the short term and the long term for both yourself and others will come."
-Dalai Lama.

"Happiness doesn't depend on any external conditions; it is governed by our mental attitude."
-Dale Carnegie.

According to psychology, an attitude refers to a set of emotions, beliefs, and behaviors towards a peculiar object, person, thing, or event. Attitudes are outcome of experience or upbringing and they have a powerful influence over behavior. Attitude some time acts as a measuring scale to evaluate people and things. Your demeanor will always tell people how you really feel about them and this will influence your happiness. When I tell someone that I am happy with your performance, it's not my words but my feelings or attitude towards the person that will communicate whether I am happy for him!

Let us take an example: If you say sorry to someone, the other person can judge whether you mean it or you are doing just a formality. **John c Maxwell rightly said, "People may hear**

your words, but they will feel your Attitude". Attitude can be formed from a person's past and present experience. We often hear the phrase, ***"Happiness is an Attitude."***

Happiness attracts people with the right attitudes as per psychology; when we're happy, our breathing becomes seamless. We find world so beautiful, consider people and things very positively, and become more generous, more helpful, and less prone to negativity. To stay happy all the times, adopt a certain way of looking at things. It has been proved in research that an emotion is always preceded by a pattern which is collection of unique thoughts linked to that emotion (Happiness, Love, and Anger).

Try framing right patterns of behaviors for your emotions and delete bad patterns which are hampering your productivity.

Do frame the right attitude for a happy and prosperous life.

ASSERTIVE

“No one can make you feel inferior without your consent.”
-Eleanor Roosevelt.

“The only healthy communication style is assertive communication.”
-Jim Rohn.

We all are expressing ourselves since childhood to convey our needs and show our point of view. I recall my childhood; we are three brothers and among them I am the eldest. I never used to demand for anything and was obeying all instructions as given by my parents, whereas the brother younger to me was very aggressive and he used to manage to get what he wanted at any cost but was not my parents’ favorite. The youngest of us was very clever. He used to express his demands in such a way that parents happily agreed to his demands and he used to get things as per his choices. I always used to be overburdened despite being in their good books. At that time, I didn’t understand why I could not get anything of my choice. Despite obeying and doing everything they asked of me whereas the youngest brother used to enjoy freedom and that “favorite son” tag with his smart work. Now with time I could associate that these were

3 different methods of communication. Mine was submissive, a 'Yes' man. The 2nd brother was aggressive, not interested to hear anything while the winner was youngest with his assertive communication.

We can keep our point of view in simple words in front of anyone without hurting that person and that is the assertive approach of communication. It has been considered the best approach of communication adopted by most successful people. Behaving aggressively, we do not allow others to communicate and deny their rights. While being submissive, we compromise our own rights. When we communicate and behave assertively, we acknowledge our own rights as well as the rights of others.

Assertive communication is an open honest communication while listening to other person and understanding their views. Assertive people don't indulge in conflicts and if stuck sometime in such situations, they can easily handle them gracefully. Assertiveness increases our self-confidence and reduces fear and stress from our daily lives. Most important thing about assertive approach is that it maintains love, respect and harmony which are the basic ingredients of a good relationship and happiness.

You can very easily say no through your assertive approach, reducing a lot of conflicts and saving time to be more successful. **Be assertive in your life, stand up for your rights and things to enjoy more happiness and success.**

ADAPTABLE

“Adaptability is not imitation. It means power of resistance and assimilation.”
-Mahatma Gandhi.

“It is not the strongest of the species that survives, nor the most intelligent that survives. It is the one that is most adaptable to change.”
-Charles Darwin.

Rightly quoted by Darwin Sir, adaptability in your nature is the only thing that will ensure survival in the constantly uncertain and changing world. Adaptability is the basic benchmark to maintain relationship and stay happy and successful in competitive world. Have goals and plans in life but be flexible to change them according to the situation and practicality. When we resist a change or situation, gradually it becomes too big to be handled and may scare us and make us stressed. Adamancy is a sign of weakness whereas adaptability makes us strong and powerful. Let us take an example: There is a change in leadership in your office and you are very much attached to your previous boss. The principle of adaptability suggests that you should not resist but accept the new leadership to continue contributing effectively and growing. In case you resist, you may feel anxious and may find it difficult to work and grow. Whenever there is a change, the first thing you will have to do is to be open-minded, observant, analytical and unbiased. When you adapt to the situation and are ready to accept the changes, it creates flexibility in your personality.

Adaptable behaviors are popular both at the house and workplace. Adaptable attitude keeps you away from conflicts which can be major cause of unhappiness. This adaptive approach will increase your efficiency and chances of success. If you have failed or missed some opportunity, this adaptive behavior will help you quickly recover from the situation and allow you to start afresh with more zest and alacrity and no baggage of the past.

Keep changing the mode of transport you use to travel, keep changing the restaurant you go for outing, keep changing your diet, keep changing the dress codes, keep changing the music you listen, keep changing all that are 'changeable'. This small activity will generate a greater level of flexibility in your behavior and you will be more, versatile, happy, and successful.

> **"In our lives, change is unavoidable, loss is unavoidable. In the adaptability and ease with which we experience change, lies our happiness and freedom."**
>
> **-Buddha.**

✣ ✣ ✣

CHAPTER 2

B OF HAPPINESS AND SUCCESS

BELIEVE

"You don't become what you want, you become what you believe."
-Oprah Winfrey.

"There's no sense in going to a tournament if you don't believe that you can win it. And that is the belief I have always had. And that is not going to change."
-Tiger Woods.

Believe in self and get away from everything that stands in the way of what you have planned to accomplish in your life. There is a very good saying - **"You can or you cannot, in both the cases you are right"**. It depends on your beliefs. Moreover, if you don't believe on yourself, then nobody else is going to believe on you. The biggest myth is someone else can make us happy. I could be happy going to some place, meeting any person, or buying a particular car. These are some examples wherein we are under the trap of an illusion, that something external will make us happy. No one else's love or approval is a substitute for your own. Only you should permit yourself to be happy. If you are not fond of yourself, you cannot truly love anyone else or appreciate the love that is given to you. Other people can bring meaning and happiness into our lives, but it's a prerequisite that you learn to depend on yourself first. The belief that other people have everything better and the grass is green the other side is wrong. In today's social media driven world, it is easy to get the wrong idea about other peoples' lives. It has been proved by research that people create an illusion that they are doing phenomenally well but the reality is entirely different.

Everything happens twice in life once in mind and secondly in reality.

Rightly quoted by Tiger woods - 'Going to a tournament without having the belief that you are going to win is of no use'. Similarly, all celebrities and sportsperson who have achieved niche in their career, believed that they are going to achieve it. Else it would never have become possible for them to reach the place they are at right now. If you are planning to crack an entrance exam, have a belief that you will definitely triumph it, then only you can. If you are planning to win a medal in sports, believe that you will get one. Similarly, if you want to earn money, have belief that yes definitely! Then only is it possible.

The mantra here is having a strong belief that you are going to achieve what you have decided for yourself and nobody other than you can stop you. **Believe in yourself and you will be happy and successful.**

✣ ✣ ✣

BEHAVIOUR

"Human behavior flows from three main sources: Desire, Emotion and Knowledge."

-Plato.

"Good behavior doesn't have any monetary value. But it has the power to purchase million hearts."

- APJ ABDUL KALAM.

I have read so many books and conclude that there are no bad people only bad behaviors and behavior is a function of two variables: values and environment.

Values are the beliefs which you develop in your childhood by observing your family and friends whereas environment is the atmosphere which surround us. It is bit difficult to change values, but we can easily change our environment to make necessary changes in our behavior. Creating a good environment around us will attract lot of positivity, be it your house or office. If you are stuck in a bad state, change the place and environment. You will immediately get rid of your problems and sense a positive change in your behavior.

Happiness requires action and everyone has different

preferences in terms of what makes them feel happy, activities will be individualized. You may find fun in a long drive whereas I prefer meeting a friend over coffee. To be happy, we have to identify patterns and habits which are hampering our efficiency and affecting our behavior.

Let us take an example: If you always reach late to office and have developed a habit of reaching late, this needs to be rectified, as it is going to be soon reflected in your behavior. If you regret something after doing it, then again, this habit needs to be checked as it is going to lower your self-confidence and decisive power. Over and above, your daily habits play a big role in determining your general mood. Repeated negative feelings impact how you feel about yourself and the world around you. Think of the habits you'd like to change by doing self-introspection.

We are all guilty of having unhealthy habits. What matters is your ability to identify and gather the courage to modify them into more positive, beneficial behaviors. **Display a behavior which you would like others to exhibit make necessary corrections if desired to stay happy and successful in life.**

BREAK

"Take a break and give your soul what it needs."
-Audrey Kitching.

"The best therapy is just taking a break."
-Dr.C.K. Kantiya.

Sometimes, we need to step outside our workplace, home, or study room whatever it may be to get some fresh air and thank god for giving us such a beautiful life. Breaks allow us to appreciate the beauty of nature and revive our mood. Breaks can increase efficiency and improves the quality of work. *Have you had ever pondered over why a period in school or college is kept of 40-45 minutes?* Answer is simple, as humans lose their interest and concentration after this time, so how can we expect happiness without taking breaks in life. Keep on taking breaks at regular intervals to stay motivated. Breaks can also be useful to get out of stuck states and for better decision making. Whenever we are in stuck state we are at loss. The best way to handle this is to break the state, move away, change the environment, and stop thinking. Plan holidays at different location on regular intervals, take a BREAK from regular food to stay healthy and improve your immunity. Keeping a break from food in the form of fasting will also help in self-healing power of your body.

A break helps us to maintain optimal stress levels; not too much and not very less. This is what we call **Eu stress** and that is good for increasing productivity and happiness levels. Breaks also help us to become more innovative and creative. *Taking a break enables us to create connections that can help addressing the topic we want to convey. It allows our conscious mind to engage with something while permitting the sub-conscious mind to work continuously in the background on the topics that we are struggling.*

Keep taking regular breaks for regulating emotions, staying fit and be more successful.

❖ ❖ ❖

BUSY

"If you want to conquer fear, don't sit home and think about it. Go out and get busy."
-Dale Carnegie.

"Success usually comes to those who are too busy to be looking for it."
-Henry David Thoreau.

The root cause of unhappiness is over thinking or unnecessary thinking which happens when you sit idle. Keeping yourself busy all the time is the ultimate key to happiness and you will get rid of over thinking and stress, the main barriers of unhappiness. Keeping yourself busy is very important as we all know that our mind never sleeps and while wandering here and there it may take you to a place which is not desired. Empty minds and free people are very dangerous and destructive. Being occupied, we keep our mind and body active for better efficiency and constructive results and in this manner; we reach close to our end goal. Busy mind aligns all energy to complete the end objective and are less exposed to anxiety and other mental health issues. The reason is very simple: All mental health concerns occurs due to over thinking and sitting idle. Busy people don't have time for contemplation and isolation which make them mentally strong, that is paramount for a happy and successful life.

Let me share you an example: Most of the retired people who don't plan their post retirement life, start considering themselves old and after some years they attract some sort of diseases. Whereas those who plan their post retirement, keeping themselves busy in their dreams and unfulfilled desires, look younger, happier. In many cases, I have seen people perform better in their second innings. Similarly, if you do not keep your cars moving, after some time the battery of car may die and after couple of months of not using, the engine of car may start stop working. Mind, body, and engine never gets tired by keeping them operational but they start malfunctioning when kept out of work. When you are busy, you won't have time to get perturbed about idle thoughts; you sleep better and feel more confident and motivated. **Amitabh Bachchan Sir, Superstar of Millennium is the quintessential icon to understand the importance of having hands full.** He keeps himself wrapped up in one project or other, still looks active and young even in late 70's and is an ideal role model for many, including me.

Busy people are organized, disciplined and work as per priority which increases chances of success. It not only applies to the working people but also to housewives and students. People who stay immersed in different tasks tend to be happier than idle ones.

Set your goal drive hard to achieve it by keeping yourself busy all the time and staying like a dog with two tails.

✣ ✣ ✣

BE BETTER

"The goal is not to be better than the other man, but your previous self."
-Dalai Lama XIV.

"Every Day set a goal to do something new, to make it better than yesterday."
- Dr.C.K. Kantiya.

Happiness and excitement in life becomes low and less as and when we, stop listening and behave as if we know every thing. Being better is the mantra of Junior Chamber International which is a group of young and Dynamic Leaders and Entrepreneurs with which I have been associated for past so many years and have learned lot of things from it .The tag line of JCI ***"Be Better"*** is the best thing which actually has transformed my life in a big way which clearly states 'to keep on improving, keep on making yourself better.'

No one in this world is perfect and there is always a scope for some improvement. The path of betterment and improvement is the path of real happiness. When you accept that you can be better, you start giving gravity to opinions, feedbacks and suggestions given by friends, family members and colleagues.

All the champions and superstars of world always try to be better than their last record. One Powerful sentence which I love to listen from champions saying ***"Best is yet to come."***

So, what about you and me? Can we say that we know everything and we are perfect? **I think 'NO'**. We can look at our daily routines and make so many things better than yesterday. We can be fit, more organized more disciplined, more composed, and more generous. Let me take an example if you are inside a room what is your maximum visibility? Roof of a Room, if you are on terrace then you can see entire house and couple of more houses in your neighborhood but when you are there in a flight looking from window outside you can see entire city. Similarly, in our life, what we see is not the complete world and there is always more to see and learn and achieve.

My message to you is break your records in terms of learning and performance you will be happier and more successful at the end. **Be better every day and achieve more out of life.**

✤ ✤ ✤

CHAPTER 3

C OF HAPPINESS AND SUCCESS

CALM

"A calm and modest life brings more happiness than pursuit of success combined with constant restlessness."
-Albert Einstein.

"The mind is like water. When it is turbulent, it is difficult to see. When it is calm, everything becomes clear."
-Buddha.

Calm mind brings inner strength and self-confidence which is very important for happiness and success. One of the best lessons you can learn in life, is to master how to remain calm. When we are happy, our face relaxes, blood circulation through the body becomes better, motivation and energy level increases. A happy person can only make other people happy. The key trait of happy people is that, they are calm all the time and if you want to be one of them, you need to be calm all the time as well.

Now the question is, how we can remain cool and calm all the time? The first thing which can help all of us, is to find some ME TIME that will help recharge and refresh the batteries of our mind. Always mean what you say. That will help you remain calm from the inside and composed from the outside. Surround yourself with good people and take full control of your life, as the moment we give control of our life to others, we are dependent on them and our happiness depends on their wishes.

Mediation, yoga and breathing techniques can be a great aid to keep our mind calm, composed and in better self-control. We should all set our limits as per our **Caliber and Appetite.** This will reduce unnecessary stress and worries. Always think before you speak. In this manner, you will be clearer and more certain about the outcome of interaction.

You are in better control of yourself, when you are clear about the purpose, sure about the words, you are going to use and certain about understanding of situation. **Be calm, composed and have full control over your thoughts and life to enjoy healthy relations, happiness, and success.**

✣ ✣ ✣

COMFORT ZONE

"Life begins at the end of your comfort zone."
- Neale Donald Walsch.

"Your comfort Zone is your danger zone."
-Greg Plitt.

A Comfort Zone is a beautiful place, but nothing ever grows there.

While your comfort area and your routines are important for creating a sense of stability and security in your day to day life, there are times when you need to learn to let go of them. If you never step outside of your comfort zone, you would never grow as a complete person. Your comfort zone keeps you constrained to limits and always stops you from doing new things. While doing something new, you might be uncomfortable at first instance, but you need to look at it as a chance to smash your comfort zone and expand limits.

'To get something you've never had, you have to do something you've never done'. Doing the same thing repeatedly will generate the same results. So, to achieve new heights of success, try doing things which you are not used to. Just try to recall the last time you tried something out of the box and the sense and feel of achievement you enjoyed on completion.

Keep motivating yourself with the visualizations and feel-good factors once you achieve the goal. Believe in yourself. Take the first step to break your comfort zone, achieve your goal and generate a smile on your face. Let me share with you an example: I was never interested for running. One day my close friend **Mr. Nilesh Sancheti** told me that he runs regularly and has finished running even Marathons. I was shocked! And he humbly told me that this is nothing great, you also can. I said, ok let me try this and in no time, I had enrolled for marathon. First time I made it 5 Km, Second time 10 and the next time 21 km Half Marathon. So, I broke my own comfort zone and I felt accomplished.

Likewise, the moment you break your comfort zone and achieve something, you feel cherished. The sense of achievement and accomplishment gives you a kick start to be happier and successful.

Daily, do something which you don't like to do. For example, getting up early in the morning or praising someone you don't like. The results will be commendable, believe me. **A beautiful world full of happiness and sky-high success is waiting for you outside your comfort zone.**

✣ ✣ ✣

CREATIVITY

"Creativity is inventing, experimenting, growing, taking risks, breaking rules, making mistakes and having fun."
-Mary Lou Cook.

"Creativity is intelligence having fun!!"
-Albert Einstein.

Creativity helps us concentrate and focus on the current moment and distracts us from worry if any. That is why creative people are happier and successful. Creativity creates a healthy state of mind. Being creative is very important to live life to the fullest. The creativity of kids, artists and advertisement people is at its best. Studies prove that being involved in creative activities will help taking anxiety and depression away from you. Activities like cooking, drawing photography, music; decoration and even doing crossword puzzles all have health benefits. **When we are being creative, our brains release dopamine, which is a natural anti-depressant.**

Creativity requires concentration that increases excitement and it generates a positive mindset. Participating in creative activities may even help to alleviate depression. Creativity gives us a sense of purpose, for living a meaningful life. There is a feel-good factor when you're being creative; it means you're doing something out of your own passion. *You're not doing something because you need to or you're forced to.* You're doing it because you love doing it and this reason is more than enough for being happy. Even if you make mistakes, while doing something you love, it doesn't really matter. The prime example of creativity is the new age startups wherein people have found doing creative and innovative ways of doing business. Creativity and innovation are going to be the next crucial differentiators in business. One of the startups which I appreciate a lot, is First Cry a portal catering to all needs of kids. How creative are they! *There is a relationship between creativity and happiness as I have seen a smile on the faces of people who are very creative. These people are less anxious, more composed better leaders and possess good problem solving and decision-making capabilities.*

Try inventing new ways of doing same task, try going with different routes to same destinations, try solving same problem with different formulae you will become more creative, better decision maker and more successful.

✣ ✣ ✣

CRITICISM

“There is only one way to avoid criticism: do nothing, say nothing & be nothing.”
-Aristotle.

“Don’t be distracted by criticism.Remember:the only taste of success some people have is when they take a bite out of you.”
-Zig Ziglar.

You may be surprised to know that there is a close relation between criticism and happiness. To understand the relationship, try spending one day without complaining and criticizing any person or thing. Continue this for a couple of days and see how your life starts changing. The complaining nature of an individual leads to unhappiness and the moment we stop complaining, happiness begins. Happiness comes from the heart and for that, you need to keep a smile on your face. Recall the last time you spent 20 minutes in your own company. Appreciating yourself, remembering your achievements, recalling the day you enjoyed in the rain while coming from school, college, or office. Recall the moment you used to steal and share lunch box in school. List out all your Achievements, Qualities and Assets and thank god for having given all this to you, thank people who have helped you out in your life. This activity will help in creating a lot of positive energy and give strength to ignore all negative people, negative energies and gradually your complaining attitude will go away.

There is a close link between complaining and criticizing. Complain is about things which we don't have and criticizing is about finding problems in others. It is easy to pinpoint the faults in others but equally difficult to correct the same. Criticizing needs lot of energy and if the same energy is used in appreciating someone, it will have positive impact on health and emotions of an individual. Always appreciate people for their good things and if they don't possess any quality which needs to be appreciated as per your definition of good, then at least don't criticize. This will not only save your energy but also retain your relationship with that person in harmony and there will be a space for future transactions.

So, for staying happy and being successful stop complaining and cherish what you have rather than complaining for what you don't have. *If someone criticizes you, accept it with a smile. If you find it worthy, then take it as a feedback, else ignore it.*

Every criticism is an opportunity to introspect, improve and do better in future. Abstaining from complaining and criticizing, will increase the number of friends you have, improve relations and lead to a happy and successful life.

❖ ❖ ❖

COMPARISIONS

“Comparison is the thief of joy.”
- Theodore Roosevelt.

“The more you praise and celebrate your life, the more there is in life to celebrate.”
- Oprah Winfrey.

Life should not only be lived; it should be celebrated. Cherish what you have instead of crying over what you don’t. Create a family of friends with whom you can share your hopes, dreams, sorrows, and happiness. The moment we start cherishing what we have God starts giving us gradually what we don’t have as he understands that you know how to care and appreciate things and are able to handle more. There is a universal law **“Give what you want”**. If you give respect, you will get it and if you trust people you will be trusted. If you want money, start spending it systematically. Gradually you will find new ways of earning it.

Every individual in this world is unique and God has specially crafted us by his own wisdom, so the moment we start comparing ourselves with others, we question God’s creation and this in no way is going to bring happiness to an individual. To stay happy, stop comparing yourself with others. We all do it from time to time. So many people get into the habit of looking at each other and comparing each other in terms of what we have and what we don't have, in terms of how happy we are with our lives and in terms of what we're doing .The biggest drawback of comparing yourself to others is that you can always find someone who is more beautiful, someone who is slimmer, someone who dresses more fashionably or someone who talks more confidently.

When you're always comparing yourself to other people what you're really saying is "I want to be more like them". When what you should be doing, is valuing more who and what you are. One of the most important things that you need to do if you want to improve your level of self-esteem is, increase accepting yourself as you are. If you can accept yourself more for what you really are, then you can live in a way that is much more honest and as a result you'll soon feel better inside. Your level of self-esteem will increase as you *stop trying to ape others.*

By not comparing yourself with others: You will be more relaxed with who you are, less stressed, confident and have a high self-esteem. Set your goal and run on your own track without comparing it with anyone else, as you may never know their struggles.

Mantra here is: *Comparisons kill creativity and fun;* celebrate what you have and enjoy because you are unique and the best version of yours.

❖ ❖ ❖

CHAPTER 4

D OF HAPPINESS AND SUCCESS

DREAM

"If you can dream it, you can do it."
-Walt Disney.

"Dream is not that which you see while sleeping; it is something that does not let you sleep."
- Abdul Kalam.

Normally we see dreams while we are sleeping and that normally is a vague picture of what we think through the day. These dreams are not of much use as they are distorted images with little meaning and way away from reality. Dreams in the real sense are thoughts that keep you moving. You start your day with an excitement and end with a review of the day and plan for next day. You don't get distracted by anything and keep on moving until you achieve the desired goal. The dreams which we see with open eyes anticipating our goals coming out true in future, are the real dreams which don't let us sleep. **If we don't start Monday with excitement and end Sunday with a party, then there is something wrong and we need to take corrective actions.** Dreams keep us lively and active and are a big mechanism of visualization. Dream takes a person to the desired state as if it is already achieved and, in this way, you get the feel of achievement.

Let me make it simple: The car you are going to drive will be the one you have dreamt of sometime. The house you are going to reside will be the one you have dreamt of and the job you are going to do will be one you have dreamt of and finally the status of life you may be living will be the one you have dreamt of. Dreaming is an important attribute of big business tycoons as it allows them to expand their thinking without putting any restrictions.

Dreaming allows you to anticipate your future and do necessary arrangements to achieve the desired goal. Dreams will let you live your dream life. **Dream Big, Achieve Big and be happier and more successful in life as stated by Dhiru Bhai Ambani.**

DECISION

"The Decision you make today will determine the stories you tell tomorrow."
- Craig Groeschel.

"It is your decisions, and not your conditions, that determine your destiny."
-Tony Robbins.

The Success and happiness of an individual pivots on a very important attribute of personality that is decision making capacity of an individual. To be happy, decide and choose what you must do for yourself, instead of others deciding for you as what to do. Your control on your decisive power, ownership for the purpose escalates your confidence. Confidence plays a vital role in decision making and if you are confident enough to take good decision and take stand on your decisions, you will always be happy and more successful. Decisions can be termed good if they are made prudently and thoughtfully considering all available alternatives.

Good decisions are those which are not only good for an individual but a win-win for all. The decision you take after Class X^{th} whichever stream you choose may be science, arts or commerce based on interest, undoubtedly would make a big difference to your life and career. This one decision of yours, will decide your career. The decision to do a job or become an entrepreneur based on your background and risk-taking appetite will also be very crucial. The decision to marry a right person will determine happiness for rest of your life. Taking right decisions at right time with right people will determine your happiness and success. Before taking any decision, jot down the pros and cons of various options and do a *SWOT* analysis. Good decisions and astute attitude will differentiate you from others in terms of happiness and success. Decision of when to speak and when to keep silence, decision what to say when to say, decision of whom to deal with and whom to ignore, decision where to stop and when to go ahead all these help in constructing a strong personality.

Astuteness or acumen is an integral part of one's personality. Simplest strategy to take a good decision is flip coins because when the coin is in air you suddenly know what you are wishing.

Take right decision at right time to attract more happiness and success.

DIARY

“I can shake off everything as I write; my sorrows disappear, my courage is reborn.”
-Anne Frank.

“I love to write my diary because in my tough time sad pages give me strength and good pages give joy to overcome from that situation.”
- Wordscrawler‘BP’.

Planning is very important for accomplishing any task. Diary may really act as a wonderful tool for happiness. Unplanned and unorganized things normally give a lot of pain whereas planned and structured things generate good results. Diary can help you record what you wish to do and what exactly you want to do in the coming months, years and even rest of your life. I started keeping a diary since my childhood. I used to write good and bad experiences of my life in that diary. One day while sitting at home, I read one of my old diaries and I calculated whatever I wrote on the first day of that year as targets and resolutions, 50% of that I could achieve. I could understand one thing clearly if I write something it means, I really need that thing and I put my serious and sincere efforts to achieve it.

Diary writing can be a very important tool for happiness and success. Writing helps you release many emotions and keep your heart lighter. As you write, you release your anger, frustrations, and all harmful thoughts. When we write goals, our subconscious mind starts working on it by framing and forming strategy to achieve the target. Make diary writing a part of your life. This will make you more disciplined, happy and target oriented. Keeping a daily diary helps in recording your varied daily experiences, noting down ideas for future reference. Diary acts as a tool to learn about yourself; that means how you think of yourself, what exactly you want in life, what are your priorities for the day, for the year and for the near future. Finally, diary can transform your life. It can furnish your problem-solving skills, reduce the stress in your life, whet your memory functions, lose weight, or make you more reticent and resilient. Whatever you want to do, keeping a diary can help you to keep your mind focused and determined to achieve the goals that you have set for.

Each new day is a blank page in the diary of your life, do write what you wish to achieve. **Maintain that diary, review it on regular basis and then see what wonders in terms of happiness and success, it does to your life.**

✣ ✣ ✣

DIET

"Dieting is the only game where you win when you lose."
-Karl Lagerfeld.

"If it came from a plant, eat it.If it was made in a plant, don't."
-Michael Pollan.

A powerful statement I read in a Sports complex "30% Gym 70 % diet Abs are made in the Kitchen not in the Gym" now I think the word diet is making a real sense here. Diet must do a lot with mental health and happiness just recall a day when you went out for a party and ate and drink whatever you wanted to, the next day you wake up with a heavy head. When we intake fruits and juice we feel fresh. Heavy lunch and fatty diet make us lazy and it proves the statement we are what we eat. Our bodies also respond according to the foods that we eat and digest daily. Eat healthy and energy giving foods and your body will thank you in a positive way by providing you with more energy which will lead to a greater sense of happiness in your life.

When we fill our stomachs with refined sugar, artificial sweeteners, and processed food, it leaves us tired and cranky. In contrast, healthy food helps reduce depression and boosts our mood. The first step towards a balanced diet is becoming aware of your diet, body, and job. For example, if you have an office job and it hardly involves any physical workouts, then it is better that you avoid food having more fats and include healthy diet. If you are in a job which involves lot of physical activity, then your chances of having fat deposited are very less. To keep control on your diet there needs to be a process which must be followed. Eat less than your hunger, give proper time to chew the food, reduce intake of Sugar and Salt. The roots cause of all the health issues in this world are these two things :Sugar and Salt. Salt impact your blood pressure levels and sugar increases the probability of diabetes. Junk and canned food are not at all good for health.

Try to be a vegetarian as origin of most of viruses which have spread across the world come from animals. Recent example of the same is Corona Virus. Your looks in public are the outcome of your diet which you take in private.

Go with nature, eat what is naturally available and is easily digestible by our digestive system to stay happy and live a prosperous life.

DISCIPLINE

"Discipline is the bridge between goals and accomplishment."
-Jim Rohn.

"We don't have to be smarter than the rest. We have to be more disciplined than the rest."
- Warren Buffett.

The distance between dream and reality is called discipline and it is necessary for achieving happiness and success. Disciplined people can fly freely anywhere by keeping a control on his emotions. It is within our powers to do what we don't feel like doing, so, it is our responsibility and duty that is important not our feelings. The struggle and pain associated with doing something which we don't like is momentary but the pleasure and gain of it are long term and much more beneficial. Sometimes the price of a small extra effort is too less to unlock the treasure of success.

If you really want to inculcate discipline in your life, learn from Army personnel. I was in a camp with one of my friends Pracheesh during my holidays. When I went to bed, the person who was taking care of tent where I was staying, asked me what time would you like to have breakfast in the morning. I said 8, thinking maybe he will bring the same around 8.30 or 9 as it usually happens in civil life. To my surprise, he was there sharp at 8, and not a single minute's delay, with my breakfast. I was impressed and afterwards I realized the importance of discipline and its impact. That is why our Army is considered the most disciplined Army in the world. Even the TV and the radio commercials are designed with utmost discipline and punctuality. You can check this; even the numbers of seconds are fixed. For example, even a few seconds more in an advertisement means much higher cost.

Discipline is an integral part of all the schools, wherein every class period is structured and everything is synchronized. There is a discipline of dress, about what to wear on which day. Gradually as you move up to higher classes and become casual about studies, the academic results also stop coming as per the desired expectations. **Those who continue to practice this habit of discipline in their lives achieve greater benchmarks of success and stay happy.**

✣ ✣ ✣

CHAPTER 5

E OF HAPPINESS AND SUCCESS

EGO

EGO=1/KNOWLEDGE

"More the knowledge lesser the EGO, lesser the knowledge more the EGO…"

-Albert Einstein.

"When the ego dies, the soul awakes."

-Mahatma Gandhi.

Your ego is the image you have of yourself.

Your social mask, the face you put on for the world, your titles, and roles: For example, that of a Father, Mother, Wife, Boss, or an IAS officer. EGO must do a lot with happiness. It is a big hurdle between an individual and his happiness. Happiness is the death of EGO. Let us make it simple, there is a big difference when we think through ego and soul. Ego always needs a purpose soul does not need any purpose, ego works from fear soul works from love, ego is based on past, present and future and soul is always in the present moment. Ego is dependent on other's action. For example, if you love me, I will be fine. If you do not love me, I am broken.

While taking any decision, if we start feeling heaviness

at heart, it means we have some constraints and we need to do some more research. Whenever your ego jumps in between the decision-making process say loudly thank you for the information and please keep silence for some time. One more interesting fact that we should all know, is that there is a close link between intuition and happiness. When we are inspired, we are happy even when problems are coming in our way. For example, when a student has set a goal of securing first position in the school, he is ready to go through any pain. He may be studying for long hours, cutting down sleep for many days, with the inspiration to become the topper helping him lift all his obstacles. When we're inspired, we're trusting that everything is okay and that there is something beautiful and wondrous about life. The mantra for happiness and success is to know what inspires you and what keeps you consistently inspired irrespective of all odds. You go for so many massages, be it head, foot, body. Try one more i.e. an ego massage in which you must leave your ego and take care of other person's ego. You will be happy and attain more success in life. Ego massage is my terminology of not hurting anyone and conveying messages assertively without getting into any conflict.

Concisely, ego controls our happiness and we may conclude that ego lives in a virtual world which has no actual existence.

***Your ego is something you have to live with, but you don't have to listen to it* or believe what it has to say and when you leave your ego behind and start the search of your own soul, which is actual "YOU", that is when you will attract happiness and more success.**

✣ ✣ ✣

EXPECTATIONS

"My happiness grows in direct proportion to my acceptance, and in inverse proportion to my expectations."
-Michael J.Fox.

"Peace begins when the expectations end."
-Buddha.

Lower expectations make it more likely that your outcome will exceed expectations and will have a positive impact on you. Let me share you an example I normally get good yearly appraisals. But to my shock, one of the appraisals was not up to the mark which broke me completely and I felt very much frustrated. I am thankful to one of my friends, who made me understand the situation. That it is not the result which has shattered you, but the expectations which have made you frustrated. My learning from that incident was great, which has always helped me in keeping a control over my expectations.

Do your best and expect the least, whatever comes out will always give you a reason to smile. According to my experience, an expectation is one of the many reasons of unhappiness. When people and result don't come as per your expectations, and then starts the frustration. When we have expectations, we are giving the trigger of our happiness in someone else's control. Let us take another example: If you expect a promotion and you don't get the same, you collapse. If you expect a gift on your birthday and you don't get it, you become disheartened. If you expect an appreciation for your work and you don't get it, you become sad. If you expect love from someone and you don't get it, you become disappointed.

As per the Holy Book Geeta "**Do your best and don't expect**" *is the happiness mantra whatever you get in return is a bonus that will increase your happiness level.* **This new approach of working wherein you reduce your expectations, taking higher ownership of results will increase your efficiency and the probability of getting success.**

EXERCISE

"We do not stop exercising because we grow old - we grow old because we stop exercising."
-Dr.Kenneth Cooper.

"It is exercise alone that supports the spirits, and keeps the mind in vigor."
-Marcus Tullius Cicero.

Nature has designed our body to work, to move and to do various physical activities. Do you know what happens to something you don't use? Yes, that's right; you tend to lose it.Example: Battery of your car when you don't start it for a couple of days. Do exercise regularly, in whatever form it may be like a morning walk, using stairs instead of lifts wherever possible and yoga or may be swimming. Regular exercise releases dopamine into the brain, the chemical that is released into our brain which is a catalyst for producing happy feelings. Research has shown exercise as one of one of the best things you can do to trigger dopamine into the brain.

Making the equation simple: The more you exercise, happier you will feel at the end. Life these days has become very hectic and most of us find it difficult to do exercise on regular basis, but those who exercise regularly have more energy levels and less stress. There are countless studies that have proved that increased exercise is directly proportional to reduced stress level. The people who exercise regularly and do workout have better physique and possess higher degree of self-confidence. You'll be amazed at how your self-esteem levels and confidence in your appearance can increase over time due to regular exercise. Exercise improves immune system and reduces risk of depression and anxiety. *There is a significant link between lack of physical activity and mental illness. A good workout is a great way to clear and flush your mind.*

A good workout is what you hate doing, but you love finishing. **So, keep doing exercise in your daily life in some form or the other to stay fit, happy, and successful.**

❖❖❖

EMPATHY

"The path to gaining respect is paved with knowledge and empathy."
-Evan Brown.

"The opposite of anger is not calmness, its Empathy."
-Mehmet Oz.

Empathy is seeing with eyes of another, listening with ears of another and feeling with the heart of another. Empathy can really make you happier as it is feeling someone else's pleasure by stepping into his shoes. In this manner you become part of the event, making the other person feel important and concerned. Empathy has broadly two parts: first is a mental part and second is emotional. The mental part is the ability to put you in the mind of another person and to see the world through his eyes whereas the emotional part is caring about what the other person feels and experiences .You could be the richest person in the world but may not be the happiest, if you don't have friends and family to share your experiences, feelings, achievements and emotions. If you can't empathize, you can't have loving and long-lasting relationships.

Paying attention to others and listening them with

desired attention is a tremendous gift to them. In this way, you become better at reading other people's signals, feelings, body language and become empathetically sound. Individuals have a very powerful capacity for empathy. Empathy allows us to make a connection with others by recognizing their values and understanding emotions. Empathy can be learnt very easily from children, as they do it naturally, due to which they can talk to strangers and interact without any pre-defined notions. They trust them and do things for them without question.

People having good public relationship and social acceptance are more empathetic towards others. **Being empathetic ensures good relations at home as well as at workplace.**

❖ ❖ ❖

EMOTIONAL INTELLIGENCE

“Emotional Intelligence accounts for 80 percent of career success.”
-Daniel Goleman.

“When you welcome your emotions as teachers, every emotion brings good news, even the ones that are painful.”
-Gary Zukav.

Controlling and managing our emotions is important as they are the key driving forces for our happiness. Our body and mind accept things in original which means whatever you feed in; they will accept no right no wrong. It is our thinking and mindset which gives meaning to these inputs. Emotional intelligence has nowadays become a chief variable which acts as a differentiator for success and leadership. Emotional quotient is another factor which decides employability and adaptability of an individual. People who are emotionally intelligent are more suitable candidates for various key positions in corporate industry. It is the key to being an effective leader and a critical factor to the quality of both our personal and business relationships. Emotional intelligence is directly proportional to our quality of life, level of ecstasy and degree of self-satisfaction.

People who have a high degree of emotional intelligence can manage feelings like anger, happiness, insecurity, or fear in a better way in contrast to those having lower degree of the same. Studies show that as much as 80% of the average person's success, in both their personal life and career, can be attributed to their level of emotional intelligence. This means that as little as 20% of a person's success is because of their IQ. People with good EQ are more Self Aware, have better control of their emotions, more socially aware and are more engaged. Emotionally intelligent people improve the quality of their relationships, cultivate leadership skills, and garner the respect and love of others, all leading to ebullience. So, a person with emotions in control is the happiest person as he does not let emotions to lead the show, which means keeping a balance of anger, excitement, achievement, and failure.

In all situations, emotions in control will minimize the effect and hence maintain an overall harmony in body, soul, and mind. **Develop your Emotional intelligence or learn from leaders who are good at it to stay happy and achieve more success in life.**

✣ ✣ ✣

CHAPTER 6

F OF HAPPINESS AND SUCCESS

FAITH

“Faith is taking the first step, even when you don’t see the whole staircase.”
- Martin Luther King Jr.

“You must not lose faith in humanity. Humanity is an ocean; if few drops of the ocean are dirty, the ocean doesn't become dirty.”
-Mahatma Gandhi.

Faith is just like a Wi-Fi, invisible but with the power to connect you to your need. Faith and Success are directly proportional to each other. If you have faith in yourself, you can do anything. Let us take an example: While walking on a road in a dark night, you keep on walking without knowing what is next on the path. Why? The answer is simple because you have the faith that you are moving in the right direction and are on the right path. Having faith in your dreams, goals and yourself is of paramount importance, as without faith, success is not possible. Faith means you never quit on your dreams, your goals, and the pursuit of your main purpose in life. People having faith do not allow anything to get in their way.

Faith enables you to overcome every obstacle in your path towards success, howsoever difficult it may be. Without faith, there will be doubts and disbelief, which lead to non-performance and insecurity. Faith draws and attracts what you want into your life, whereas doubts and disbeliefs push them away. Faith, feelings, desire, and positive thinking are essential for achieving success in addition to action, will-power, discipline, and persistence. We cannot drive cars without faith, how could we fly on airplane without having faith on pilot. *Faith is as important as the air we breathe and helps us discover purpose and solutions to various problems of life.*

So, to stay happy in life, have faith in yourself, have faith in your Parents, have faith in your Friends, have faith in God, have faith in the Universe, you will be exultant.

FEAR

"We grow fearless by walking into our fears."
-Robin Sharma.

"There is no illusion greater than fear."
- Lao Tzu.

Fear is an illusion. The chance of its happening is very rare but it mars our happiness and present moment. We may have a fear of success, fear of failure or fear of losing someone. We can keep a check on it and take correct actions if we understand our own inner truths. It really needs courage to introspect and find out who you are and what exactly you look out of life. Sometimes it may be bit scary but it is okay to be scared. If you let that fear rule your life, you will always remain unhappy. It is wrong to believe that the safe way, the easy way, the approved way, will make you happy, but it won't, it will only make it safe and easy for you to be unhappy.

Winning the approval of others for happiness is an example of inner fear and low self-esteem. Your fear of being happy is perhaps the number one obstacle that we tend to put in our way. Remember that being happy is different from taking happiness for granted. The common threat is the fear of change and uncertainty. Most of the time, when you are waiting for "The right moment", the motivating fear behind it is one of these two: either you are scared that you will fail, or you are afraid that you will succeed and will not be able to handle the massive success.

For example, if you are appearing for a competitive exam, the first fear is I cannot clear the same. And even if clear, I may not be able to clear the interview. Even if I clear the interview, I may not able to settle away from my home town. Now looking at this example you can very easily understand that all these apprehensions are ridiculous and you are just wasting your time thinking about all this stuff. You never know what you can achieve unless you take the chance and try. 90% of the fears will never appear in real life so it is always better to face the fear and deal with it rather than avoiding it to get away from it. *As Roosevelt quoted "All we have to fear is fear itself."*

A fearful person can never be happy and will hardly be able to achieve anything great. Mantra here is living a fearless life.

✣ ✣ ✣

FORGET

“Forget the Past.”
-Nelson Mandela.

“Forget those things that aren't worth remembering.”
-Tim Foley.

Our mind is like a smart phone; if there is low memory or multiple applications opened simultaneously, it gets hanged or may crash after some time. Similarly, our mind may also not be able to function properly or be stuck, due to lot of unnecessary memories and bad experiences which are creating hurdles in learning new things and obstructing us from working efficiently. What do we usually do to repair our phone? First, we close unnecessary apps running in background and delete pictures, applications and videos which are not of use any more and then restart the phone. The same exercise we will have to do with our mind as well: Forget all those people, places and things which are creating hurdles and, in this manner, we create space for learning new things, storing fresh experiences, and then increasing the performance of our mind. Forgetting all the things which are of no use or which are distracting you from your work or your present will make you happier and lighter at heart.

Let go those harsh emotions from your past and that will keep you refreshed and rejuvenated. This activity will help us in greater inner clarity and state of well-being and help with learning and remembering easier. Forgetting is like a mind flush to remove all toxic chemicals from mind. If we cannot forget, gradually it also impacts your memory. I have forgotten all the people whom I don't like, I have forgotten all the experiences which created panic in my life, I have forgotten all the places with which I have had bad memories. *Keep flushing your mind to delete bad memories and creating space for new so that you can cherish the good things and stay happy and successful.*

Mantra here is forgetting things and experiences which are pulling us down but never forget your purpose of life and reason to live.

❖ ❖ ❖

FORGIVE

“The weak can never forgive. Forgiveness is the attribute of the strong.”

-Mahatma Gandhi

“Mistakes are always forgivable, if one has the courage to admit them.”

-Bruce Lee.

Forgiveness is internal process of letting go of feeling and thoughts of resentment, bitterness, anger, and revenge for someone whom we believe has wronged us in some way. Forgiveness is the ultimate measure to generate internal peace; a pleasure feeling in our heart when we let go our grievances. Forgiveness is a positive action of taking responsibility for how we feel in the present moment and find a way to become hero in our own story rather than becoming a victim of the other person. LETTING GO makes you more powerful and wiser to move forward in the direction of achieving your goals.

Pardoning reduces your blood pressure, stress, anger, heart rate, anxiety and on the positive side, it increases friends, improves relationship and psychological wellbeing. Learning to forgive has many proven benefits, including freedom, optimism, strength, and purpose to treat others the way you would like to be treated. The courage to forgive is stronger than the fault committed by someone. Forgiveness is not something we do for other people. We do it for ourselves to get well and move on. I have forgiven all the people who have hurt me, I have forgiven all the people who have cheated me and I have forgiven all the people who have caused financial losses to me.The act of forgiveness makes you feel light by clearing undue grudges and creating a great human being in your own eyes with enhanced self-respect.

> ***"To err is human; to forgive, divine."***
> ***-Alexander Pope.***

The mantra here is to be happy and successful keep forgiving people and don't hesitate in saying sorry if you think that will create peace, space, and harmony in your own life.

✣ ✣ ✣

FRIENDS

"You can make more friends in two months by becoming interested in other people than you can in two years by trying to get other people interested in you."

-Dale Carnegie.

"A friend is one that knows you as you are, understands where you have been, accepts what you have become, and still, gently allow you to grow."

- William Shakespeare.

Friends are lifeline of happiness and it has been universally proved that people having a good friend circle enjoy a balanced and healthy life. We need someone with whom we can share our problems, feelings and celebrate good times. Our personality is greatly influenced by our friend circle knowingly or unknowingly. In other words, you are an average of the friends you spend your most of the time. So, if you want to improve your individual average, you need to surround yourself by good friends. They will act as motivators helping you grow in life.

Psychologists have found that people are happier when they are with friends in contrast to when they are alone and happy people are more sociable. This creates a direct equation between happiness and sociability. Being in the company of people makes us feel happier, and again, being happier makes socialize more. They found that those who connected with more people felt more positive and happier. Spending time with your friends makes you happier than spending time with anyone else of your close relationships. The mantra is straight: Have as many friends as you can, connect with strangers may be on morning walk, inside a mall or while you travel. Share your happiness with friends and ask their achievements and help each other in the time of need. *Our friends help us live longer too, and if you don't trust this, take a visit to a nearby public park. You will see groups of old age people surrounded by so many people who look younger and happier with a smile on face than those few sitting alone on benches.*

Friends are the fuel of life without which it is very difficult for you to stay happy and get more success in life.

✣ ✣ ✣

CHAPTER 7

G OF HAPPINESS AND SUCCESS

GOAL

> **"If you want to be happy, set a goal that commands your thoughts, liberates your energy and inspires your hopes."**
> **-Andrew Carnegie.**
>
> **"Setting Goals is the first step in turning the invisible into the visible."**
> **-Tony Robbins.**

Goal creates a road map and blueprint for success and acts as a source of inspiration. The more precise and accurate we are in our blueprint, better are the chances of achieving end objective. Goals give a starting and endpoint to reach the ultimate destination. Goals help you focus on the purpose and avoid unnecessary distractions. Successful people always set goals in all areas of life, be it spiritual, physical, financial, social, and professional that will empower you to live your vision with more power.

When I was in college, my teacher told me, *"If you want to be really successful, find out what God wants you to do with your life and then dedicate yourself to achieve it"*. At that time, I didn't really like the idea. I did not believe that my life could have any particular purpose. Gradually, with age and experiences, I realized that my teacher was right. According to Maslow's theory of Psychology as human beings, we all have certain basic wants and needs: food, water, shelter, safety, love, respect, and self-esteem. Every human being tends to move from pain to pleasure and uncomfortable to comfortable. Somewhere along the line, I came to realize that what God wanted for my life and what I wanted, were the same thing. So, finding that real purpose of life is finding goal of life. Life without a goal is like a train without engine going nowhere.

Goal must be decided with a deadline. Everyone should have a purpose in life i.e. Goal. Goals give clarity of that end objective, what exactly you want out of life. They keep the fire inside on, allow us to keep on moving, allow us to stretch our limits and makes us more accountable and responsible. For example, setting a target for weight loss of 10 kg in 10 months makes you aware of what to eat, what not to eat and by when to achieve the desired result.

My message to you is simple, it is time for you to wake-up. It is the time to set a purpose of life. It is time for you to set goal for your life. It is time for you to fulfill your dream-however difficult that may be. **We are here on this planet with a purpose; by finding your own unique purpose in life, you will be living your dream life full of fun excitement, happiness, and success.**

❖ ❖ ❖

GOD

“When the solution is simple, God is answering.”
-Albert Einstein.

“Believe. You are never alone; God is always with you.”
-Catherine Pulsifer.

God has a valid reason for everything in this world to happen. We may never understand His wisdom but we simply must trust His will to stay gratified and achieve opulence. Different religions have different Gods to follow or trust no matter what is the name of GOD, if you go by literature - God is a single universal power known as almighty. This almighty is same for all casts, creeds, and communities. Now the link between God and happiness is a matter of concern. If you have faith in God, it means you have faith in yourself and you are calmer, more composed, and balanced. These are all the characteristics of a happy person. So, we can say that person having trust in God is more likely to be a happier person. If you don’t believe in God, start believing, as this will not only boost your self-confidence but also broaden your mindset to look at things. You will accept situations and things at their face value and will start appreciating circumstances, believing it might have happened for something good and god might have better plans for you.

Many of my friends wanted to be something in life but couldn't become what they wanted. Initially they got frustrated and depressed but the moment they accepted that god might have planned something better for them, things started working on their way. Let me share example of one of my friend Vijay Pal who could not clear PET in Multiple attempts and was feeling very low for some time, about to give up. Then he accepted that god might have better plans for him. He joined engineering Diploma and finally completed his Engineering degree in lateral entry. Today he is settled in US with a happy family. Faith in God or a universal power will usually get you through the toughest of times. Look up to this HIGHER POWER to develop faith. This faith will keep you in a state of happiness. *The trust in god not only keeps your values high but also makes you a better human being, who is kind enough to help people and contributes to the society in some form.*

Success mantra is accepting situations, putting consistent efforts and belief in god. People who believe in GOD are happier and tend to get more success.

GRATITUDE

“Gratitude is the healthiest of all emotions. The more you express gratitude for what you have, the more likely you will have even more to express gratitude for.”

-ZIG ZIGLAR.

“If the only prayer you said in your whole life was, ‘thank you,’ that would suffice.”

-Meister Eckhart.

Studies have proved that practicing gratitude increases positive emotions, lowers stress, increases satisfaction, and refines relationships.

Say “thank you” to God. Say thank you to your parents and say thank you to everyone around. Researchers have proved that writing and delivering a gratitude letter has a positive impact on happiness. You can respect your work and value your body for being capable of executing the duty. You can be grateful for your home, family, and friends. You can give thanks to your life for just the way it is. The ‘Vibration’ of gratitude attracts more positive things in life. It’s amazing to understand how one small simple activity can change so much in a person’s life.

One of the things that have had the biggest effect on my life is the realization of the power of gratitude. I was lucky to visit ***"ISHA Dhyan Kendra"*** established by great ***SADGURU*** during one of our official travel. I spent one day there and the best thing which I learned from there was gratitude. There used to be an activity wherein you need to thank all the Directions, Sun, Moon, Stars, Mother Earth and then all the people present in the session. It was such a powerful activity through which any negative state and bad day can be converted to a good one. To overcome a bad phase, make a gratitude list and instead of getting mad at someone, show gesture of gratitude.

Choosing gratitude over criticism will improve existing relationships and open door for new. **Mantra here is to attract happiness and success make gratitude an integral part of your personality.**

❖ ❖ ❖

GENEROUS

"Generosity is giving more than you can, and pride is taking less than you need."
-Khalil Gibran.

"If someone doesn't smile at you, be generous and offer your own smile. Nobody needs a smile more than the one that cannot smile to others."
-Dalai Lama.

Generous people are normally contented people!

These are the humans willing to share their time, possessions, and talent for the benefits of other. I remember a powerful statement: miserly you become poor, generously you become rich. To stay happy, always be Generous and Gentle and find joy in giving, by giving you get to gain even more. The habit of giving opens a new link to receive things of our need. Generous people are more relaxed and love to work hard as their focus point is not self but the other person whom they wish to make happy. We can say generous people are more result oriented rather than being self-centered.

ALTRUISM makes people more confident and they carry better relationship at home and workplace. This characteristic of their personality makes them more successful. When people experience the beauty of giving, they'd want to give back too, so what goes around, comes around. Try sharing the good things in your life for which you are happy, it might be possible that what you have others might not have; may be an art, may be some information or may be talent. Get in the habit of donating things you don't need any more. For example, old clothes, textbooks, books, toys, and the like. I do it on regular basis. Normally we keep ourselves confined to our own world. So, either we are very hard or very demanding, try bringing out the gentle side in you for a change. It'll make you a warmer person to be around.

A successful person is one who has tasted the joy of giving, who has understood the joy in giving and persists on giving. **This attitude of generosity with which a person feels accomplished and satisfied in giving is the real sign of elation and prosperity.**

GRUDGES

"Life is too short for long-term grudges."
-Elon Musk.

"Grudges are like hand grenades; it is wise to release them before they destroy you."
-Barbara Johnson.

Holding a grudge is like drinking poison and expecting the other person to die. Grudges are biggest enemies of happiness. To live a grudge free life, laugh when you can, apologize when you are wrong, let go of what you cannot control and keep a smile on your face. Learn from your mistakes but never regret. People change & things go wrong but always remember, life goes on. It is about what is important for you. The problem with grudges is that they don't serve any purpose neither do they make us feel better nor heal our wounds. At the end of the day, we end up as owners of our grudges. Hence disconnecting us from our own heart. Resentments have a negative effect on both our mind and physical wellbeing. Grudges reduce our immunity and healing.

The path of freedom from grudges requires two step

strategies: First, forgive people with whom you hold any sort of grudges and secondly, increase your love for everyone. By changing the perspective of looking at things, we will gradually develop a better mindset. The best way to release grudges is to meditate regularly and read holy books. Looking at things from other person's perspective, we take a better position to release the grudge and understand the overall angle for holding the same. Change in mindset improves self-awareness and self-control, so we develop empathy for others which will help in releasing the grudges. While holding grudges, you keep thinking of some past event and person but all successful people live in the present. Living in the present is possible only by releasing grudges and by stopping dwelling on problems. Holding grudges affects creativity, develops stress, and reduces the probability of success.

Simple way of releasing grudge is to write down everything on a piece of paper; whatever happened with you and what you expected and finally to accept the reality and tear this piece of paper and throw it away in a dustbin. Imagine the agony vanishing from your heart and the venom released when you tear the paper. A new soothing feeling of kindness and compassion can be realized.

Live a grudge free life for happiness and more success.

CHAPTER 8

H OF HAPPINESS AND SUCCESS

HERO

"Be a HERO always say, I have no Fear."
-Swami Vivekananda.

"A hero is someone who has given his or her life to something bigger than oneself."
-Joseph Campbell

We all are fond of watching movies be it Bollywood or Hollywood. The most important character whom we love to watch is the Hero. The spotlight is always chasing one person in the entire movie, the Hero. To become a hero in real life, list out your strengths and weaknesses. Write your life goals and assess what is that which is keeping you from achieving your goals. Find the lacuna in the form of increasing your strength and removing weakness. To be a hero in real life, you will have to study great personality's life stories and need to inculcate the change you want to see in others.

You can be a hero for your family by scheduling everything starting from the time you wake up, exercise, diet, and the way you carry yourself in day to day life. You may not be conscious about the fact that everyone at your house learn a lot from you. You cannot expect discipline from your kids when you don't follow the same. We all can be hero by helping our kids achieving their goals may be sports or academics, helping our parents fulfilling their desires of visiting religious places or may be contributing in building our society by giving donations or helping the needy. *When we live playing the role of hero in the movie of life, the spotlight is always on us and we give our best. How can you expect a hero to do an unhappy and unsuccessful role, right?*

Do play the role of a Hero in the reel of life every moment to be confident, result oriented, healthy, happy, and successful.

HARDWORK

"There is no substitute for hard work."
-Thomas A. Edison.

"Success is no accident. It is hard work, perseverance, learning, studying, sacrifice and most of all, love of what you are doing."
-Pele.

There is no shortcut to success; hard work is the only key to success, a powerful statement that I have been listening to, since my childhood and I found it very apt in my real life. Hard work teaches us discipline, dedication and persistency which are the basic building blocks of success. When we work hard, we learn lot of things and get novel experiences which at the right time of time make us a smart worker. My school teacher used to tell us that there is nothing free in this world or you can say there is a price for everything. Hard work is the price you pay for becoming successful. Hard works gives you an advantage; it is a tool to build confidence and self-improvement. The people who achieve success through handwork always carry values and they are more ethical that makes them happy overall. I recall a very good Hindi Proverb **"Karat Karat Abhyaas key Jadmati**

Hout Sujaan Rasri Aawat Jaat Te Sill Par Parat Nissan." which means regular efforts will give good results like a rope can create impression on stone, whatever tough may be a task, regular efforts will make it simple.

Happiness and success do not come on a silver platter. There needs to be sincere efforts. Along with increased mental toughness, hard work gives you the chance to improve yourself. Hard work will help you develop self-discipline and focus. In turn you will become more efficient and productive. I *have heard interviews of so many IAS officers who hail from villages and hardly had any resources or money to support but one thing that was common in their life, was hard work which made their success possible.*

Key to success is rigorous hard work and the sense of achievement will make you triumphant.

HONESTY

"No Legacy is so rich as Honesty."
-William Shakespeare.

"Honesty is the Best Policy."
-Benjamin Franklin.

Honesty can help you in all corners of life; be it happiness, work, relationship and above all success. Honesty is the best policy; across the globe. Remember the Nursery Rhyme **"Johnny Johnny Yes Papa telling lies no Papa"** so lies will not take you long but honesty will help you grow. The more honest you are with yourself, the more comfortable, happier, and successful you will be. The quality of honesty will not only keep you mentally fit but also physically fit. Honesty also improves your personality as people can understand what type of person you are and they also feel comfortable in your company. It's a spiritual truth that true happiness requires honest self-reflection. The more honest you are with yourself, the greater happiness you will experience.

Being veracious brings about an inner ease and happiness and in other words there is a congruency in your words and body language. Honesty in yogic terms can be defined as a congruency in what we speak, what we feel and what we do; when we feel out of alignment it is usually where there is a conflict between what we think and what we feel. When we aren't honest, we feel anxious, disturbed and less confident. The greatest honesty lesson I have learned is from my father who is a retired Army Officer and he cannot be mendacious. Feels strange, doesn't it. Yes, it is. He faced lot of challenges in his job, personal and social life because of this honesty. Even I used to tell him sometimes to give in and speak lies wherever desired if it is beneficial. But then he used to explode on me. Now when I see him at the age of 73 getting up at 4 'O' clock in the morning, still young and active, looking as if he is just in late 50's, no stress, no anxiety no disease, living life like a king. Even most of his colleagues are no more, those who are there, are in very bad health. The secret of all this is only one word his VERACITY towards self, towards his work and towards the society.

The truth makes it is easier to live life in original and being yourself. **Let us make it simple, be honest to yourself, love yourself, be what you are and live a happy and successful life.**

❖ ❖ ❖

HEALTH

"It is health that is real wealth and not pieces of gold and silver."
-Mahatma Gandhi.

"Health is like money; we never have a true idea of its value until we lose it."
-Josh Billings.

We see the world from our state of mind. If we are happy inside, we are happy outside which means however good or soothing may the climate outside be, you will not enjoy it if you are not healthy, mentally, and physically. So, health must do a lot with our happiness and success. We take care of our belongings, we take care of our near and dear ones, we take care of our investments but we ignore one very crucial aspect of our life, that is Health. As rightly said by legends, health is actual wealth and we cannot expect happiness in an unhealthy body. Every human being is the author of his own health or disease. Many of us simply do not get enough sleep which leads to weakening of our sensory acuity, muscles, and concentration levels. On top of this, our weakened state can lead to health concerns and deep feelings of tiredness and unhappiness throughout our day. Go to sleep only when you are tired and wake up at the same time every day. This will undoubtedly lead to much more satisfaction and happiness in your life.

Research has proved that happiness and health are closely connected and one's level of happiness can impact the level of one's health. Happiness protects your heart, strengthens immune system, and reduces stress. Happy people have fewer aches and pains.

A Healthy Mind dwells in a Healthy Body. Keep yourself away from toxic things and people, toxic things can be any sort of addiction; smoking or drinking and even toxic people who are the negative and experts in finding mistakes in everything.

Mantra here is whatever you eat, whatever you drink, whatever you speak, whatever you do, always keep in mind that it should be good for your health. **Happiness lives around health and healthy persons have better chances of attracting happiness and success.**

HOPE

"Hope means keep going, thinking, 'I can do this'. It brings inner strength, self-confidence, the ability to do what you do honestly, truthfully and transparently."
-Dalai Lama.

"Hope is being able to see that there is a light despite all of the darkness."
-Desmond Tutu.

Don't lose hope, when the sun goes down, the stars come out.

The very purpose of our life is happiness and that is sustained by hope. We have no assurance about the future, but we exist in the hope of something better. Hope strengthens or supports that state of happiness. When we as individuals make plans, we may feel empowered, happy, excited, and even hopeful for a time. In 1991, the eminent positive psychologist Charles R. Synder and his colleagues came up with Hope Theory. According to them, hope consists of agency and pathways. The person who has hope has the will and determination that goals will be achieved and possesses a set of different strategies at their disposal to reach their goals. In simple words, they have the will and purpose to get there and different ways to get there.

Hope makes learning simple and improves performance, which directly elevates the confidence and increases creativity. Hope can give us valor, strength, and audacity instead of fear. Hope increases endurance and patience which are the prerequisites to achieve success. Cricket is the best example to understand hope; both the players and audience sitting in the stadium never lose hope till the last ball, as many a times the match becomes a last ball match but the team and captain who maintain the hope comes out as a winner at the end. We could even say that the only constant in this world is change; this should not be a cause of despair, but rather a ray of hope. Hope keeps you zealous all the time and improves your overall psychological health.

Being hopeful is an art and may act as a starting point of happiness and success for most of us. **Let us all give our best using available resources and always be hopeful that best is yet to come.**

❖ ❖ ❖

CHAPTER 9

I OF HAPPINESS AND SUCCESS

INTEREST

> **"Interest is the root of knowledge."**
> **- Abraham Joshua Heschel.**
>
> **"If you always do what interests you, at least one person is pleased."**
> **- Katharine Hepburn.**

When we do something of our interest, we don't feel like work is a burden as we enjoy doing that work. The excitement and thrill of doing work when we do work of our interest generates power within to accomplish the task. I love talking and interacting with people. So, I never get tired doing this. Let me share with you an example: It was the last day of March, quite late in the evening when I was planning to leave. Suddenly my senior asked me to prepare a report. You can imagine my state of mind, my visage, and my countenance but I had no other option but to say yes. Now I did something that I was not interested. So, there was no excitement. Next month same closing activity happened but this time when I was about to leave my boss came to me and told me that we all are going for a late-night party and will celebrate success. Everybody said yes with excitement and there was no stress, fatigue, boredom, and sadness though everybody had worked for the entire day. So, see the paradox in these two situations, it is simple in the first case, I was not interested. so, I was knackered and there was no excitement and thrill but in the second case, everybody including myself were enthusiastic and excited as a party was something that everybody was interested and ready to do. So, there is a big learning from these two incidents; fatigue is always mental, never physical. It is our mind which controls our body. When we are interested in doing something, we never feel boredom and tiredness. We love to do it increasingly as our mind drive it increasingly and when we are not excited to do something, mind resists and it hampers the overall efficacy.

So, in life those who are fluky, get jobs of their interest like singers, musicians, cricketers and actors. They all set new records breaking their own and are remembered by millions for years because of their contributions. The innovation and achievement of one's niche is possible only when we are doing work of our interest and we can easily find these people happier than their counterparts.

Mantra here is: to stay happy, do a job of your interest if this is not feasible and possible then develop some interest which keeps you excited. May be Running, Sports, Singing, Writing or anything which really gives you a kick. This kick is a trigger which is none other than your interest.

FONDNESS for your work and attitude of being interested in the others will keep you happy and successful for long run.

❖ ❖ ❖

INTEGRITY

“In looking for people to hire, look for three qualities: integrity, intelligence and energy and if they don’t have the first, the other two will kill you.”
-Warren Buffett.

“When you are able to maintain your own highest standards of integrity-regardless of what others may do-you are destined for greatness.”
-Napoleon Hill.

The word integrity comes from the Latin integrities, meaning wholeness. In simple words practicing what you preach. Integrity has been considered an important parameter of human personality globally one needs to exhibit both at workplace and home. It includes the genuine presentation of oneself to others as well as the internal sense that one is a morally coherent being. The antonym of integrity is deceitfulness and insincerity. The biggest benefit of integrity is that it allows us to modify our behavior so that we can be more efficient in our lives. There is an affinity between integrity and happiness. One cannot be happy if he lacks in personal integrity which means not being completely honest to self in all areas of life be it personal, professional and academics.

Lack of integrity is one of the key causes of stress and unhappiness and what is more surprising; it has never been mentioned as a cause of stress in most of the literature. When we maintain integrity and honesty, we feel very good and calm with ourselves and there is a perfect self-alignment with ourselves. Whereas when we are not truthful, we invite stress which blocks the full feel of human happiness. Dishonesty and lack of integrity is biggest roadblock to the path of happiness. Being honest to self will set us free from our own mental and emotional prison. Integrity can be made an integral part of our personality by some simple techniques. First thing is to stop telling lies to your friends, even passing fishy compliments and sharing false stories of your life just to put an impression, though you know that it has no resemblance with real life. Secondly keep a check on the number of times you tell lies on daily basis. This frequency should reduce day by day.

To sum up, happiness is not a knowledge test. ***It's an integrity test and this is exactly what I refer to as integrity.*** **The more you are integrated with self, brighter are the chances of staying happy and living a successful life.**

INSECURITY

"Most bad behavior comes from insecurity."
-Debra Winger.

"It's Insecurity that is always chasing you and standing in the way of your dreams."
-Vin Diesel.

Insecure thoughts keep us miles away from happiness and badly impact our entire well-being. Insecurity is a state where you are not sure about your future or thinking too much about uncertainty may be financial, emotional, or psychological. The root cause of insecurity is low self-esteem and insecurity is a chief ingredient of upcoming unhappiness. Insecurity can come from your own self-judgment or from the judgments of others. I remember the days of my college life when I was about to finish my degree. I did my graduation and post-graduation in IT but the time we were about to pass the degree, there was a recession and a high sense of insecurity. People used to get placed but chances were huge that they may be kicked out in a short span. So, I was in a big dilemma what to do and what not to do. The insecurity was in terms of getting a job and surviving in the industry being a fresher. Due to improper guidance and handholding, I decided to leave the main stream IT and choose something which was a mix-up of IT, admin and teaching and joined an IT Management Institute which was again a bad decision I made, which I realized later.

One day I decided to remove this sense of insecurity and it came to my mind that now onwards I will work on my skill set and talent which is never going to vanish and nobody can steal. Gradually law of attraction started working and I cleared audition in AIR for FM RJ and I realized my core strength, which was eloquence. I started enjoying my Job and hobby as an RJ. Sense of insecurity started drifting away from me as my self-esteem started aggravating and confidence level was also higher. Later, a lot of offers started coming in a year. I tried my hand in corporate industry. I got a chance to get into corporate training and then the journey of security and happiness started since then I am enjoying my job and I am passionate about it.

The purpose of sharing my experience was to demonstrate the need of removing insecurity out of life. You don't live your dream life when you are surrounded by negative thoughts and feeling of insecurity. Get rid of insecure thoughts to be happy and simplest technique to handle them is to get aware of them, identify them, and take corrective actions. *Work more on your skills and talents to get rid of feeling of insecurity.*

Set realistic goals and stay in company of positive and successful people to be happy and successful.

INTUITION

"Intuition is a very powerful thing, more powerful than Intellect."
-Steve Jobs.

"Intuition in chess can be defined as the first move that comes to mind when you see a position."
-Viswanathan Anand.

It is important to know what inspires you and what keeps you consistently inspired irrespective of all odds. Intuition in simple language can be understood as gut feeling or the voice of soul which guides you all the time and stays with you all the time. Recall the day while coming out of an examination center; you know how many marks you are going to score without any external feedback. Some people have higher intuition knowledge or we can see that they are better connected to their souls. We use GPS to find some location and maps to locate some areas but there is no guide or map to understand our mind, so intuition is very much required.

To remain happy, you need to follow your gut instinct, let your intuition guide you you'll never go wrong with it. The more you follow your gut, the stronger is your connection with your intuition. We can change our life by looking from different perspective operating through intuition normally termed as sixth sense apart from 5 senses which exist to receive inputs to our mind. Whenever we go for a new job offer, a new relationship or a new opportunity our ego comes into action but what needs to be believed and followed is our intuition. Using intuition as a guide will make decisions better and more accurate as it is our direct connection to soul. Normally we try to seek happiness from outside materialistic things but this happiness will not last long as it is just a source of pleasure. Internal self-satisfaction will generate long term happiness. Let me share another example of working through intuition: I was at Indore during my post-graduation when Radio Michi was launched. One day while listening radio I was really impressed by the person who was live on radio and wished if I could be one. After my studies, I returned to Jodhpur there was a gut feeling that I will certainly come on radio some day and that was my inner voice, the voice of intuition. I followed the Intuition and became a FM RJ.*So when you really need something and are interested in, your intuition will act as a guiding map to achieve what you have decided to do.*

Any goal or intention that comes from your heart is not only truly genuine, but it happens effortlessly when you follow the guidelines of your own intuition.

❖ ❖ ❖

IGNORANCE

> **"To succeed in life, you need two things: ignorance and confidence."**
> **-Mark Twain.**
>
> **"Knowledge Is Power, Ignorance Is Bliss: Happiness is striking the perfect balance.**
> **-Paul Hudson.**

This is an apt statement wherein we may interpret that knowledge gives you power and authority with the help of which you can grow establish and settle in life at a good position.

The real secret of happiness which comes into application is Ignorance, giving attention to anything and everything will lead you nowhere as you need to be bit choosy and smart enough to focus on events and information which are useful to you and may add value to your life. Unnecessarily focusing on some events or persons will waste your time and invite lot of other problems. Let me share you an example: There is a person in my office who carries a rigid religious and political ideology and whenever I try to give some logics and share my point of view, he becomes aggressive and rebellious. As we must interact for some reasons or other for official concerns, he always brings in his ideology and beliefs and we always end up in a bad notion. He had been enjoying making me irritated by imposing his ideology and creating a nuisance, but it used to drain a lot of positive energy of mine for no use. Finally, one day I decided to become *oblivious, ignorant,* and not to indulge in any discussions with this person. Things started changing in a big way; I could give my message without creating any dispute simply by becoming ignorant. I started saving lot of positive energy and my self-control also increased in this way I made him realize his mistake also, by being oblivious.

Life is a cycle. The more we live, more we experience and more we learn and this way we gradually create a sense of wisdom to decide what needs to be given emphasis and what needs to be ignored. So not knowing information that causes us pain and leaves us worse off is obviously more pleasant than knowing that information. Will you prefer to remain ignorant to things and persons that cause pain?

I would recommend: To be happy and more successful in life, ignore the negative voice inside your head instead focus on your goals and remember your accomplishments. We can avoid majority of our troubles in life if we ignore irrelevant things and information which are not meant for us as in that way, we save lot of time and positive energy which otherwise would have caused lot of stress, fatigue, and misery to us with no end results.

There is a powerful statement: Weak people seek revenge; strong people forgive and intelligent people ignore.

You can be happier and more successful using the power of ignorance wisely.

✤ ✤ ✤

CHAPTER 10

J OF HAPPINESS AND SUCCESS

JOB

"Choose a job you love, and you will never have to work a day in your life."
-Confucius.

"Doing what you like is freedom. Liking what you do is happiness."
-Frank Tyger.

If you love your job you need not to love again and this statement is very apt as far as relationship of Job and happiness is concerned. It is not the job or work which makes you tired it is the type of work or interest in work which makes you tired. Happiness is mostly a choice; you can choose to be happy at work or spend whole day criticizing. Though it sounds simple, it needs some effort to put it into action. We all wish to have the best employer in the world, but let's face it, we may not. Think positively about your work and enjoy your work look at the positive side of job as there are so many people in this world who are jobless and you are lucky enough to have a job or Business. When you are in a job which is not of your interest start finding positive things in it and start working parallel, in area of your interest. Let us take an example if you work in sales but that's not your real flare, you wish to work in academic industry so acquire qualifications which are necessary for working in academic industry. When you acquire the necessary qualification, you can try your luck in your favorite industry. In this manner, there is a *motivation inside* which will *increase your efficiency* in the existing job and keep you happy, excited, and motivated to find a new job of your interest.

In short, if you are positive, all good happens to you whereas a negative mindset at job may also impact your health and working. Find coworkers you like and spend your time with them. Your choices at work largely define your experience. You can choose to be happy at work, you may or may not love your current job and you may or may not believe that you can find something in your current job to love, but still you can. I am writing this book during corona pandemic. I remember many of my friends who left jobs and started their own business in the field of training. Now since everything is locked and we are being stuck in lockdown for many months, first time I have realized importance of working for a good brand.

Cherish your job; give your best to stay happy and successful

JUDGEMENTAL

"Thinking is difficult, that's why most people judge."
-Carl Jung.

"If you judge people, you have no time to love them."
-Mother Tersa.

There is a great learning from Buddhism, in which they do an activity of holding a strawberry; when we can comfortably look at the strawberry without seeing whether it looks good or bad, without seeing the impact of its color or anything else, we can then move on to something larger. May be a meal or a subject and finally, when we are comfortable with all of this, we will be ready to try it out with humans.

This simple activity teaches us to learn how we can treat people, places, and things naturally without being judgmental. In this manner, we will gradually start accepting things in their original form and thus increasing chances and probability of greater success.

Let us take an example: Whenever you see a boy and girl walking together, what is your first reaction or opinion about their relationship? If you pre-decide about this relationship, it means you are a bit judgmental. Else if you wait for some more information and communication, then you are not. Whether you are judging or being judged, it's time to better understand its long-term impact, so that we can better let it go. We normally rate our own worth based on how other people perceive and look at us. Being judgmental causes a lot of opportunity and professional losses.

Let us understand it with more examples: If you are prejudiced about a particular community, you will respond to any person of that community based on your perception. In this manner, you may suffer losses commercially as well as personally. If you are judgmental about a particular gender, then also you may look at that gender based on your experience, which may impact your relationship badly. If you are judgmental about some place, then you might miss a great sightseeing experience.

> ***"Be Curious not Judgmental."***
> ***-Walt Whiteman.***

Treat every person as unique, every place as an adventure and every experience as fresh without being judgmental to cherish the new world full of happiness and success.

❖ ❖ ❖

JEALOUSY

"Jealousy is a mental Cancer."
-B.C. Forbes.

"Envy is the art of counting the other fellow's blessings instead of your own."
-Harold Coffin.

Jealousy is the art of counting someone else's blessings instead of our own.

You may be surprised to know that jealousy which is a complex human emotion can make you insecure in your relationship, job and may affect your happiness in a big way. Jealousy is a constant state of fear for the future and a constant state of demands and need. The more you are demanding, more are the chances that you will compare yourself with others. When you aren't satisfied with what you already own, when you aren't appreciative of the people in your life, or are constantly searching for the latest and greatest, these fantastical images of a life someone else is living can result in comparison, which will eventually translate in self-criticism, self-doubt, and insecurity.

Jealousy is a symbol of insecurity and you are not satisfied with who you are or what you have. At the end of the day, your opinion of yourself is the only one that matters. Jealousy makes you self-seeking and could negatively affect your performance at work and satisfaction level. Jealousy prevents you from being a more mindful person and there are some tips to keep jealousy away from our personality. Primarily, take control of your emotions and avoid reacting at all the things and situations that will save lot of time and energy. Always take some time before framing an opinion. Identify your core beliefs that are the starting point of jealousy by becoming aware about yourself. Finally take control of your attention as happiness and success do not reside where jealousy and envy dwell. *Happiness is a journey, not a destination. So, treasure every moment you have and remember that time waits for no one.*

Replace *the word jealousy in your dictionary with appreciation and feel the difference which you may realize in your life.* **Your friends, relatives and colleagues will start getting attracted and concerned towards you and this will make you happier and bring greater success in longer horizon.**

❖ ❖ ❖

JOKES

"The Best ideas come as jokes. Make your thinking as funny as possible."
-David Ogilvy.

"A day without laughter is a day wasted."
-Charlie Chaplin.

In today's scenario, life of every person has become so busy that they don't get ample time to enjoy and relax. Stress levels and mental health concerns are increasing day by day leading to compromising hectic schedule, poor lifestyle, and improper food. Jokes play a vital role to ease our lives and play the role of panacea to relieve our stress. The importance of jokes is that when people around you are either sad, in a serious mood or in a problem, jokes can help them to feel better. Jokes are normally one liner or stories that bring laughter to the people who are listening. Joker is the only character in entire circus who not only attracts kids but everyone in the mob. You know why, as everyone wish to laugh and remain happy. Laughter is contagious and it activates our all senses to generate a pleasure feeling. Happiness in other words is laughing at self.

Psychologists have found that persons who can crack jokes and love to enjoy jokes possess better mental health and were more sociable than other people. So, keep reading good jokes and don't spare any opportunity to crack a joke appropriate to the situation. A joke makes us laugh and impacts our body in a positive manner. When we start to laugh, it not only just lightens our body but also induces many physical changes in our body. Funny jokes boost up the human immune system by increasing infection fighting antibodies. Laughing impacts blood circulation and help in heart and other cardiovascular problems. Jokes increase endorphins, released by brain helping to reduce pain and help in relieving our anger, depression, tension, stress and make us feel light and irritation free without anxiety and fear.

Jokes are mood boosters having social benefits at workplace through which we can impress our customers, colleagues or business contacts that indirectly helps us in cracking good business deals. Jokes sharpen our sensibilities and tune our capabilities and hence improving our personality by bringing out lighter side. Humor also allows people to express their feelings without any hesitation. *Laughter through jokes can help changing perspective to handle any difficult problems or issue in just minutes.*

Mantra is Jokes if practiced not only increases your happiness level but also improves your communication skills.

✣ ✣ ✣

CHAPTER 11

K OF HAPPINESS AND SUCCESS

KNOWING YOURSELF

"Knowing yourself is the beginning of all wisdom".
-Aristotle.

"Life is never made unbearable by circumstances, but only by lack of meaning and purpose."
-Viktor E.Frankl.

Finding yourself and knowing yourself is paramount for happiness. Seriously think about what you want out of life. We attract what we think and we are inclined to focus more on what we don't have. So, we get away from what exactly we want.

Let me *demystify* it: We ponder a lot about what we don't want instead of concentrating on what we do. Knowing what we want is fundamental to finding ourselves. Recognizing our wants and desires help us realize who we are and what's important for us, recognize your personal power. When we know what we want, we are challenged to take power over our lives.

"Personal power is based on strength, confidence, and competence that individuals gradually acquire in the course of their development," said Dr. Firestone. Knowing our personal power helps us in a big way.

We create the world we live in and to create a better world means shifting our outlook, feeling, and rejecting all negativity and victimized approach towards life. Decide goals and take proactive actions to achieve them. You better understand yourself when you are open to new ideas accept constructive criticism. **Mahatma Gandhi once said, "The best way to find you is to lose yourself in the service of others."** *Who we choose to surround ourselves with has a profound effect on how we relate in the world?*

Always be with someone who makes you smile, never compromise on your values, think positive, do what you love to do, live life for a purpose, listen voice of your heart, break your records and always welcome changes. I know that I am at peak of my ability and capability in the morning hours and become very dull in the late evening this knowledge about me helps me to prioritize my work accordingly. I complete the vital things in the morning slot itself so channelizing my energy accordingly. If you know that you don't like people with mind set, its better you keep yourself away from them else you may get into some trouble.

> ***"He who lives in harmony with himself lives in harmony with the universe."***
>
> ***-Marcus Aurelius.***

Knowing your preferences, thinking patterns and areas of interest will help you in being more focused in achieving your goal and maintaining an optimal level of satisfaction and happiness.

❖ ❖ ❖

KNOWLEDGE

"An investment in knowledge pays the best interest."
-Benjamin Franklin.

"The light of knowledge can never dawn on the proud."
-Mahatma Gandhi.

The only discriminator between two humans is the intellect which they possess. Knowledge is now an integral part of a human personality. It may be difficult for you to change your looks, height, weight, and your society but the easiest and most relevant change we can make in our lives is that we can escalate our knowledge to increase understanding of things, happiness, and probability of success. The best example of this is a boy who may be born in a slum but he can become an IIT'ian or IAS Officer through hard work and knowledge. So, knowledge can make a big change in anyone's life style and earning. The employability of an individual may increase manifold by acquiring knowledge supported by relevant academics. If I make it simple, the starting package of a Graduate from a normal institution and an IIT may vary manifold, the differentiator is qualification with appropriate knowledge. I have seen many people who come from average families but have become millionaires simply through their domain expertise.

Knowledge about health, people, environment, relations, and right food may bring a big change in your life. Knowing what to talk, when to talk and with whom to talk, is crucial. Knowledge about the law, places and various career options will also decide how much success, you may get in life and how happy you stay. Knowledge gives you the power to control your future in odd times and maintain your current level of happiness because you will be prepared for any uncertain condition. The real important thing is knowledge about past that will help you to avoid the same mistakes in the future. *The moment we have knowledge about our bad patterns which we committed in past we can avoid the same mistakes again.*

Knowledge about self, others, places, and processes will give you an edge over others in acquiring success and staying happier.

❖ ❖ ❖

KIND

“When we feel Love and Kindness toward others, it not only makes others feel loved and cared for, but it helps us also to develop inner Happiness and PEACE”

-Dalai Lama.

“Kindness is the language which the deaf can hear and the blind can see.”

-Mark Twain.

Happiness can be linked to kindness, recently a psychologists’ study which was conducted over individuals across several different backgrounds, in which results seemed to indicate that acts of kindness could very well change the scope of mental wellbeing in so many different areas. Being congenial has many rewards; just look at the old proverb which states: “it is better to give than to receive.”

We should always be kind as the language of kindness is one which is universally accepted across all religion and nationalities. Like most antidepressants, benevolence stimulates the production of serotonin that can heal your wounds, calms you down, and makes you happy. Engaging in acts of kindness produces endorphins, the brain's natural painkiller which is three times more effective than morphine.

Being benevolent also produces oxytocin hormone that promotes social bonding, exerts an immediate calming effect, increases trust, generosity, strengthens the immune system, and boosts vitality. Benign people are normally less exposed to stress and are full of positivity as it reduces Cortisol, the defamed stress hormone. Be *COMPASSIONATE* to your neighbors, be *WARM-HEARTED* to elders, be *NICE* to kids, be *KIND-HEARTED* to your subordinates and be *AMIABLE* to anyone to whom you can make a difference in cash or kind. The act of benevolence gives instant results in the form of blessings .I have seen many rich people offering their kind services at religious places like polishing shoes, offering food to the needy leaving their status apart .When asked why they do so, the answer was very straight we feel happy and satisfied ,that is the power of kindness.

> ***"Kind words are short and easy to speak, but their echoes are truly endless."***
>
> ***-Mother Teresa.***

Being kind makes you more satisfied and you may achieve more success in longer horizon.

❖ ❖ ❖

KID

"While we try to teach our children all about life, our children teach us what life is all about."
-Angela Schwindt.

"Kids are like a mirror; what they see and hear they do. Be a good reflection for them."
-Kevin Heath.

Kids can be our best teachers to teach us so many things in life. As we grow in life, we leave the child inside us far behind and stop taking the things at their face value. I mean, we try to give meaning to everything we come across and associate our experience with things and people we come across. In this manner, most of the time we treat and understand people based on our perception which is a big challenge to experience the original benefit and original meaning. Kids on the other hand, take things on their face value. They do not differentiate among people; they are open to everyone. Try to make new friends and give original meaning to words, for example when you say would you like to have chocolates? They will say Yes, whereas if you ask the same question to an adult, he will try to reason that by offering anything to him, what is the real purpose behind it and link his past experience with similar situations. This example makes it clear that brooding and excessive analysis is also a barrier to happiness.

We can learn lot of lessons from kids to stay happy. Kids possess very good articulation skills and are at best at kinesics. They have a congruency in their speech which means they mean what they say and they do what they love to do. Whereas adults lack in congruency in their speech and keep different faces or masks for different occasions which make them unhappy many a times. Those who have honest communication skills as good as kids are real happy people and are more successful as this skill helps them to communicate effectively using minimal words. We can learn from kids not to dwell on the past or think too far ahead. Kids are audacious and they love to play. Similarly, we also need to be dauntless and should keep on playing some sort of games which involves physical activity. Children don't carry baggage from one day to the other. For them, each day is a fresh start. Similarly, we should work with fresh thoughts and fresh plans every day.

"Kids are very creative. "Happiness lies in the joy of achievement and the thrill of creative effort."
-Franklin D. Roosevelt.

Be creative, laugh often and enjoy every moment like kids to stay happy and attract more success. Being a kid opens mind for learning, innovation, and avenues for success.

KRISHNA

> **"Happiness is a state of mind that has nothing to do with the external world."**
> **-Lord Krishna**

> **"I have a purpose for your pain, a reason for your struggle and a reward for your faithfulness, trust me and don't give up."**
> **-Lord Krishna.**

Krishna is a real-life motivator and we can learn a lot of things from his life to be successful and happy in life. The birth of Lord Krishna took place in a prison; his parents were imprisoned without any crime! He was brought up in a small village, while he deserved to be a part of Royal Palace. Daily one or the other demon was sent to take away his life. His own uncle Kansa left no stone unturned to transform his life into hell. His own nephew Sishupal was after his life. Despite all these adversities he lived his life like a festival. He remained the same, smiling **'KANAHA'** whether circumstances were favorable or not. He remained calm even when Gandhari cursed him, or when NARAD cursed his clan. He remained calm during Kurukshetra while being a part of the greatest war ever fought. It was his wisdom because of which Pandavas emerged victorious against a much larger force of valiant Kouravas. He was so munificent that when Duryodhana asked for his army to fight against Pandavas, he gave him his whole army along with weapons.

So, what we can learn from him: Be the same "**jovial**" person in all situations. Never give up because life never ends. Do not wait for any miracle, do it yourself. Be calm and composed even when your elders are scolding you. Be clever not wicked. Forgive your foes but never forget their names. Do not leave anything incomplete. Move on in life even when your dearest one has gone forever. Do not respond to critics, just keep on improving yourself. Be ready to do anything, even break your promise if required to save Dharma. Ethics are flexible; use them for benefit of society. Be humble, even when the whole universe is your slave.

Punish them who deserve to be punished, **forgive them who deserve to be forgiven and teach them who value your teachings. The learning's of Bhagavad Geeta can revamp your life; make you** ***vigorous, dynamic, victorious, and affluent.***

CHAPTER 12

L OF HAPPINESS AND SUCCESS

LIVE IN THE PRESENT

“If you are depressed, you are living in the past. If you are anxious, you are living in the future. If you are at peace, you are living in the present.”

-Lao Tzu.

“Whenever you are in love and feel joyous, your mind is in the present. That is when you achieve yoga. The art of living lies in being in the present.”

-Sri Sri

There are only two days in a year when, nothing can be done, one is called yesterday and the other is called tomorrow, so today is the right day to love, live and celebrate the most. The point of power is always in the present moment. The biggest OPPONENT of happiness is anxiety if you want to conquer the anxiety of life, live in the moment, and live in the breath. Most of us carry this sense that happiness is somewhere out there in the future. Our hope is that we’ll find it in our next relationship, purchase, or experience. But this never happens as soon as we’ve satisfied one need another one pops up which makes us unhappy and unfulfilled.

Living in the moment really makes people happier and

this has been supported by various researches. Most of the time people are distracted from the task at hand and keep on day-dreaming either about future or cursing the past this reduces their chances of being happy. To stay happy the only way is to live in the present moment. The happiness which we get out of tangible things doesn't last long what is going to stay with us for long is the attitude of gratitude for the things we have in life. Living in the moment also ensures a Quality of work that is there in your hand. Live in the present and make it so beautiful that it will be worth remembering in future. *Living in the present moment is imperative for success; and you will live a better life.*

Despondent **people allow their minds to either dwell in the past or worry about the future and they forget to live in the present. Enjoy the moment, be appreciative and grateful for life to stay happy and achieve more success.**

LISTEN

"Most of the successful people I have known are the ones who do more Listening than talking."
-Bernard Baruch.

"One of the sincerest forms of respect is actually listening to what another has to say."
-Bryant H. McGill.

Relationships are indispensable part of our daily life and can certainly influence our happiness level. To have healthy and happy relationship we need to have good communication and a good communication does not only mean talking it includes, active listening and focus on what we are listening to. Listening can help us avoid many problems and misunderstandings. Listening can increase the probability of success as it makes us more sensible, aware, and mature. Listening expands our knowledge, reduces mistakes and helps in resolving complex problems. When we listen, we communicate respect, in this way listening increases affinity as people like people who listen to them.

Listening makes you wiser as it creates a rapport a feeling of good will in personal and professional relations. Good listening reduces the risk of misunderstandings and mistakes that could otherwise be very damaging to personal and professional relationship. There are so many people who speak so well but the number of good listeners is in dearth. Those who are good at both are the real champions socially popular, better settled, and successful. Listen to everyone, learn from everyone because nobody knows everything but everyone knows something. Good listeners are the best salesman, they are the best lovers, they are the best friends, and they are socially more popular and acceptable. Let me ask you a question who is your best friend one who is a good listener or one who is a good at speaker? I know the answer and you will also agree we all like people who acknowledge us and listen us seriously. Listening is not only required for effective communication but everywhere in our daily routine starting from house to office and finally in the society we live to improve personal and professional relationship. Good listeners are good learners as they observe things very minutely this make them more efficient in their working. Great leaders and preachers are very good listeners and you can very well understand their wisdom and decision-making capacity.

> ***"Most people do not listen with the intent to understand; they listen with intent to reply."***
>
> **-Stephen R. Covey.**

Always listen to understand as Good listeners choose their words wisely before speaking in this manner, they are not dragged in unnecessary conflicts making them happier and successful.

LOVE

> **"To love is nothing. To be loved is something. But to love and be loved, that's everything."**
> **-T.Tolis.**
>
> **"We are most alive when we're in love."**
> **-John Updike.**

In simple words, when someone else's happiness becomes our priority and concern, that is love.

The person who finds happiness through love is the person who can be trusted to bring happiness to others. There have been many studies that show that satisfying relationship is associated with better health, greater happiness, and a longer life. A Harvard grand study revealed that loving relationships were the key to emotional and physical wellbeing. Start by loving your friends, family, partner, colleagues, seniors, clients, teachers, and everyone around. Love unconditionally as the highest form of love is unconditional love, where you love others without expecting anything in return. A heart full of love attracts endless happiness and keeps no space for hatred.

Being in love is associated with emotions of joy and

happiness. When we love our work we don't feel like working similarly when we love someone we forget to even watch time as we are engrossed into the love of that person .Loving attitude of yours will make you very kind and socially acceptable that will also increase the number of friends you have and your well-wishers. When we love people, we look at all the good qualities of those persons in this way we are happy appreciating things people and places which generates lot of positive energy in us that is going to increase our efficiency. Love among the family members is the necessity of keeping the members intact. Marry someone whom you love not by considering the looks as after a certain age it is love which will keep you intact not the looks. Love your kids, love your parents, love your car, love your house, love your neighbors, love your colleagues, love the nature around and love everyone you come across and this will ensure more love for you from the universe in return.

> ***"Love is not an emotion. It is your very existence."***
> **-Sri Sri.**

A good reflection of love in your personality will generate more happiness and finally more success.

❖ ❖ ❖

LET GO

> **"One of the most courageous decisions you'll ever make is to finally let go of what is hurting your heart and soul."**
> **-Brigitte Nicole.**
>
> **"Letting go doesn't mean you stop caring.It means you stop trying to force others to."**
> **-Mandy Hale.**

When you develop a let go attitude, you create space for something better.

This attitude is very much needed to stay happy and successful in life. Letting go keeps your mind free from various filth which otherwise may occupy unnecessary space in your mind. Let us take an example: Is there anything in your life that keeps you awake at night? May be an experience, an incident, a lie, some regret, a bad relation or may be a secret. Let it go by sharing it with someone who is very close to you. Learn to Let it go as that is very much required to stay happy and achieve success in life. It is very much natural for us to want things in a certain way and at a certain time. For example, scoring good marks in all the classes, visiting place of our choices, finding best friends, having gadgets of our choices, and getting careers of our choices, finding life partners of choice and so on. The reality in the journey of life is that we cannot control the events but one thing which we can adopt is controlling our responses and letting go which is not in our control. We can control our reactions and responses and the best answer many a time, is letting go. We may get angry, form opinions hold grudges some time but we need to keep on doing a self-analysis, *is it worth to keep the fight on?*

Letting go of the past and accepting present will give you more freedom, happiness, and success. Let everything come to our mind as the sooner we accept what is going on better we experience freedom and peace in mind. The activity of letting go gives happiness as return gift and opens our mind to receive new innovative thoughts. We try to control everything around us but adopting a letting go strategy leaves you with what truly matters to you. That may be your soul or self-respect.

Happiness can be easily found by clearing some clutter and letting go **few things which includes let go of pleasing everyone, let go of expecting from people, let go of critics, let go of grudges, let go of ego, let go of fear of failure and let go of all negativity in this world.**

LEADER

"Leaders don't create followers; they create more leaders."
-Tom Peters.

"The best leaders have a high consideration Factor. They really care about their people."
-Brian Tracy.

A leader can bring the best out of others, who is able to inspire others to be bigger than who they are, who is able to energize people into action, who is able to lead a way with a common vision. Leadership doesn't begin when you lead a group of people; it is a part of our everyday life, starting with how we conduct ourselves and how we live our lives. Are you a leader at your home? Are you a leader in your family? Are you a leader in your friend circle? Are you a leader in your office? Are you a leader in your society? If all the answers are No, then probably you must introspect. Those who have asides' at least a few, can very well understand the privilege they feel while leading family, friends, or office teams.

Let me quote an example here; in a big corporate during interaction with top management, one of the workers made a complaint about poor condition and hygiene of toilets at work place in comparison to that of the Executive toilets. The Managing Director took it very seriously and asked his supervisor how long will it take to change all the toilets. The supervisor replied, around a month.MD said , I can do it in one day. You send a carpenter tomorrow. Next day, he instructed the carpenter to swap the signboards of both toilets. Now executive toilet was for workers and workers toilet was for executives and he ordered to continue this activity every week. The toilets got repaired and were up to date in no time. The quality of both the toilets came at par in the next three days. Leaders listen with a lot of patience and give solutions without wasting time. "The Leadership is something much more than being an Executive".

Learning from this message, Problem identification requires critical thinking, but Problem solution requires creative thinking. Be a leader in every span of life by being a solution provider in whatever form you may. Start teaching kids at home; they will accept you as leader. Try cooking a new dish and your better half will accept you as a leader. *Do act as a PARAGON in almost everything. Leaders have a purpose in everything, concentrate on solution, prioritize what is paramount and don't compare themselves with others.*

Leaders do what they say and above all they believe in themselves. So being leader in your every role will make you happy and more successful in life.

❖ ❖ ❖

CHAPTER 13

M OF HAPPINESS AND SUCCESS

MONEY

"The lack of money is the root of all EVIL."
-Mark Twain.

"If you don't find a way to make money while you sleep, you will work until you die."
-Warren Buffett.

Money does not certainly give you happiness. Rather it gives you access to many things that can lead to happiness. The first thing which money does for you, is eliminate financial anxiety and insecurity to purchase anything of your interest and liking. Money can help you buy memorable experiences be it with family or alone. Spending money will give you many moments of happiness as well as positive memories to look back on. Money will give you an access to innovative things. You can have higher level of self-satisfaction by giving charity to people who are in need. With money, we can bring smile on the many needy faces by either providing food for them or sponsoring education of such kids.

Manage your time and your expense wisely and you'll suffer less stress, worry and financial crisis. Money does not automatically make you happy but without fulfillment of basic needs of life food, shelter and safety, your world may be quite miserable. Researchers have concluded that money has a direct relationship with increased overall life satisfaction.

As rightly quoted by Warren Buffett, Money is not everything. Make sure you earn a lot before speaking such nonsense. Choose a career which will generate enough money to fulfill all your life desires. Secondly, never depend on a single source of income. Make investments to create a second source. **Earn well, invest wisely, and live a happy and prosperous life.**

❖ ❖ ❖

MARRIAGE

"Who we marry is one of the most important decisions in life. One that will influence the level of happiness, growth and success, like no other choice."

-Nathan Workman.

"A great marriage is not when the 'Perfect Couple' come together. It is when an imperfect couple learns to enjoy their differences."

-Dave Meurer.

Marriage is one of the key factors across the world strongly and consistently associated with happiness.

60% of your life happiness is dependent on that one decision - your marriage. Marriages in our country are normally considered a compulsion and if you miss out on the standard age, then lot of questions are raised. Why are you marrying so late? Even people start making lot of stories about the person. So normally the decision of marriage is taken under some sort of pressure or may be a mandatory thing or process to be complied with. In this way the selection and decision become very important as this is going to decide the fate of your life. As per my analysis, happy couples are those belonging to at least the same domain. I mean, Doctor getting married to doctor or engineer getting married to engineer. The reason behind this logic of mine is simple: After some time, the only thing which keeps marriages intact is communication and that is possible only when you have something in common to discuss. In some cases, these odd even combinations may be successful but the best combo is when husband and wife complement each other not only in their personal life but also in professional life. In this way, the probability of success and earning also increases manifold.

A successful marriage tends to make people consistently happy. A spouse can serve as a valued and trusted decision-making partner, lowering a person's stress level. To better understand the relationship between marriage and happiness, let's look at life satisfaction. Happily married people report greater levels of life satisfaction than others, and marriage can really boost a person's happiness or that sense of subjective well-being. Tips that can really make your married life excellent: There should be honest and good communication, there should not be any ego between you and your spouse, repair the arguments if any immediately, use forget and forgive strategy.

Take responsibility for your problems, avoid blaming your spouse for your problems or unhappiness, and distribute power between each other as marriages with distributive powers are the happiest.

A good marriage, happiness and success will grow together.

❖ ❖ ❖

MISTAKES

"A Person who never made a mistake never tried anything new."
-Albert Einstein.

"If you want to grow, you need to get over any fear you may have of making mistakes."
-John C.Maxwell.

Mistakes are committed by the people who do something. One should never be worried about committing mistakes as they provide an opportunity to learn. Mistakes are fundamental part of every cognitive process, whether solving a mathematical question, making important decisions, or dealing with people. Let me share with you an example: I was very weak at mathematics and used to score very less till class VIII.One day I asked my Maths teacher Mr.Monga, Why don't I get the right answers though I know how to solve the question? He acknowledged my problem and told me, that I lack practice and don't learn from my past mistakes.

It was a turnaround point of my life and I took mathematics as a challenge and in no time things changed. I am proudly sharing the fact that after that I scored maximum marks in the board exams and got national Olympiad certificate as well. Accepting the mistake and learning from it can change results in a big way. Taking complete responsibility for our actions makes us stronger and more accountable.

Mistakes make us learn; they reboot our motivation and remind us that it's all an experiment to reach the ultimate goal. We can learn from doctors who always say that they are practicing medical as a profession. They never say that they are perfect. Most of the times, doctors are successful in diagnosing and treating the patient. But perhaps, in some cases they fail to do so. It cannot be counted as a mistake, because the intention was still noble. To cure the patient. Simultaneously, doctors take it as an opportunity to learn from such shortcomings so that in future they can handle similar cases in a better manner. Wise people do not regret their past as they have learned a new learning in the class of life, while others may dwell repeatedly on their errors.

I would recommend a safe strategy wherein we should learn from our mistakes and use the past as a reference book so not to repeat the same mistake again. We may ask for forgiveness if we feel that something has been missed out from our side. This will improve our credibility and help us in becoming a better person.

Treat every mistake as an opportunity and move ahead with a smile to achieve greater success in life.

MUSIC

“Dear music, Thanks for always clearing my head, healing my heart and lifting my Spirits.”
-Lori Deschene.

“Where words leave off, music begins.”
-Heinrich Heine.

Music is the panacea for stress, concentration, low efficiency and bad mood and we can call it a language that speaks emotions instead of words. In other words, we can say that music can really play a vital role in releasing stress, improving concentration, increasing efficiency, and uplifting mood. To stay happy and enhance your efficiency, make music a part of your Life. Music should be of individual interest and one should have a good collection of music suitable for various occasions and moods. I love all types of music be it romantic, spiritual, motivational, and classic. Making music a part of our life may change the way we talk, walk, think, and act. Music since time immemorial, has been a well-tested tool for entertainment and that is directly linked to happiness. Music may be used as a mood changer tonic and makes learning simpler.

I have observed music lovers closely and one thing which was common with all of them, was that they were very calm and composed. I am sure that you will agree that a person who is calm and composed has better chances of being successful and happy in life. I have heard people talking about quality of life through branded cloths and gazettes. One more thing you can add to enhance quality of life is good music. The ease of listening to music is that it does not disturb your work. Rather, it improves the quality of work. Nowadays music is everywhere, starting from kitchen, car, office, hospitals, and clinics and even waiting areas of Bus Stops/Railway Station. Music also helps in quality of sleep. If you listen to good music before sleep, you may enjoy a sound sleep. Take some time out to listen to what makes you smile, may be in the early hours of the day or while doing a morning walk. I love **Kumar Saanu's** songs. So, whenever I wish to uplift my mood, I play the music and in just a couple of minutes, my mood changes with a lot of positive energy and fresh thoughts. Good music is like good food that gives a soothing experience and it works from the top of your head down to the tips of your toes, radiating new energy into every part of your body. Music therapy nowadays is very popular in medication and mental health diseases and for students to improve concentration. *Research has also shown that, music helps in releasing dopamine the neurotransmitter often referred to as the "Happy chemical" associated with our brain's reward system.*

Music is beneficial to our health, quality of life and acts as a mood booster to increase overall happiness.

❖ ❖ ❖

MEDITATION

"Meditation is the discovery that the point of life is always arrived at in the immediate moment."
-Alan Watts.

"Where there is a peace &meditation, there is neither anxiety nor doubt."
- St.Francis de Sales.

Meditation helps people feel more calm, clear, centered and provides a sense of wellbeing that can last all for long. People who meditate are more composed and are in better control of their emotions in all situations. Meditation increases self-awareness and connects you with your inner voice. Research has also supported the fact that those who do meditation are likely to feel better, even in tough times and unpleasant experiences. With meditation, we can change focus from inside out to outside in, to find source of happiness which lies within us and does not need any external approval. There can be less suffering when we practice mindfulness. Start living in the moment and let go of the desire to run life as per our wish. Mindfulness and happiness are closely linked as it means we're not hiding anything from anyone.

Meditation helps us to live in the present moment feel the breathings, emotions, nature, sensations, and nature around us. People are substantially less happy when their minds are wandering than when they're not, no matter what they're doing. If we practice mindfulness, we can slow down and feel the moment. Even finding just 5 to 10 minutes a day to sit alone at a peaceful place or walk in nature can help your mind become stronger and let go of all the stress and worry and enjoy the present moment.

Mind can do anything and everything and most of us are not aware about the power of mind. What it can do or what it can achieve. So never ever say I cannot do this, always say I can do this as mind believes what you perceive and it cannot differentiate between what is right or what is wrong.

Everything is right for mind and everything is wrong for mind. It has immense power and can do everything. ***"Folks are usually about as happy as they make their minds up to be."*** **Abraham Lincoln.**

Doing meditation on regular basis gives you better control of life and you may be happier and more successful.

❖ ❖ ❖

CHAPTER 14

N OF HAPPINESS AND SUCCESS

NO

> **"The difference between successful people and really successful people is that really successful people say no to almost everything."**
> **-Warren Buffett.**
>
> **"Half of the troubles of this life can be traced to saying yes too quickly and not saying no soon enough"**
> **-Josh Bilings.**

The key to happiness and success is mastery in the art of saying No. Saying "NO" to someone is the most challenging task for most of the people and inability to say "NO" is often the biggest cause of "FAILURE". Through my life experiences, one thing that I have realized is that you cannot make everyone happy in this world; if you can, you are not doing justice to your job. So instead of pleasing everyone, take care of pleasing the most important person in this world **"YOURSELF"**. To understand it better, whenever we travel by flight, the crew members make an announcement in case of any emergency, instead of helping others, first help yourself by wearing your oxygen mask.

Let us take another example: You must make an important presentation in the evening that is going to decide your appraisal for the year and suddenly your friends come to invite you for a birthday party of your close friend. Now what will you do? Most of us will say 'YES' but if we go by my theory, you should say no as this appraisal is going to decide the fate of your career for the coming year and if you think your friends are going to get angry when you say no, then it's time to review your friendship. When you say "YES" to something, ask yourself what am I giving up for that yes and at what cost are you doing. So, this will make it simple for you to decide on when to say yes and when to say no. We all have 24 hours and how you utilize this time is the key to your success and happiness. Saying NO wherever desired, will save lot of time and resources. Give yourself permission to say "NO" to anything that makes you unhappy and drains your energy.

Do regular practice of saying No and gradually you will become a better decision maker **and balanced personality who can differentiate important and unimportant thus utilizing available resources and time wisely to achieve more success and stay happy.**

NEGOTIATE

"Let us never negotiate out of fear. But let us never fear to negotiate."
-John F. Kennedy

"The most important job is that of learning how to negotiate with others without friction."
-Napoleon Hill.`

Negotiation is not just a word; it is an art and one who is good at this skill will have brighter chances of success. Negotiation is needed at all levels. Starting from personal, family life and professional life. A child negotiates with his parents to get something or to demand a toy of his choice. In return, parents negotiate to reward the kid as to offer the gift linked to some academic performance or behavioral adoption. Men negotiate in job offers and business deals whereas women negotiate in shopping so to get the best deal. So, if you are good at negotiation, the chances are very bright that you may get the best deal both in personal or professional front. I read somewhere that a big multinational shopping chain used to keep most of the price as 99,199,299,399 and so on. Prima facie, these appeared to be very attractive price as 99 sounds less, but later a study revealed that in most of the cases, they were not returning one rupee back to customers. Now imagine 5000 customers come to one store in one city and there are 5000 stores across the nation the amount which comes out is 25000000 is 2 Core 50 Lakhs in one day and if you multiply it to 30 and then 365…. So that is why, this one rupee is so important and strong. If you keep on ignoring this trifling one-rupee loss in your life, how much loss you will incur throughout your life. Now I think you can visualize how important is negotiation for success and happiness.

If you really want to be a great negotiator, listen more than you talk to ensure a win-win deal. Secondly, use timing to your advantage. Example you can get good offers on Blazers in summers and western outfits in winters. Similarly, buying a car at the end of calendar year may give a good deal and you can negotiate well. Always get when you give. For example, you are a businessman and the customer asks for discount on some garments then you must tell them to buy 2 and then you will get discount. So, in this manner, both parties are happy and deal closes on a happy note.

We may conclude that Negotiation is an important attribute required both for happiness and success.

✣ ✣ ✣

NEGATIVE

> **"Stay away from Negative people. They have a problem for every solution."**
> **-Albert Einstein.**
>
> **"Don't walk away from negative people, run!"**
> **-Mark Twain.**

Train your mind to see the good in everything as we always get that option to choose one of the two; positive or negative. The quality of our thoughts is going to decide the quality of our life. As per psychology, humans learn more from observing people around them and model the behaviors which they see around them. The best example to understand this scenario is this: If there is a charming kid at your home, the chances are very bright that there will be a pleasant environment at home. On the other hand, if there is someone in your family who is not keeping well for long, there may be a negative environment. Negative word is considered good only in the case of medical industry. For example, someone tests HIV negative or someone is tested negative for Corona.

Negative in life is not at all good, either for happiness

or for success. For example, Negative People, Negative environment, and Negative news are the biggest enemies of happiness. If you spend your time with a group of Negative people who always talk about their problems and put the most negative climax on anything they watch or hear on television or radio, probability of you turning into a negative person increases.

We all need to moderate our intake of negative news and refrain from associating with negative people. People staying together and working together influence each other knowingly or unknowingly and this gets reflected in your personality as well as emotional levels at times. We reflect other people's emotional peaks. It is better that you take charge and control of your life by avoiding people who try to bring you down into the doldrums of negativity and emotional hardship.

> **"It isn't what you have or who you are or where you are or what you are doing that makes you happy or unhappy. It is what you think about it."**
>
> **-Dale Carnegie.**

You get what you think and your language is reflection of your thoughts. **So always be positive and get away from anything or anybody who are negative, to get more happiness and success.**

❖ ❖ ❖

NUTRITION

> **"Exercise is King, nutrition is Queen. Put them together and you've got a kingdom."**
> **-Jack Lalanne.**
>
> **"The doctor of the future will no longer treat the human frame with drugs, but rather will cure and prevent disease with nutrition."**
> **-Thomas A .Edison.**

One of my doctor friends Dr.Ajay Pal Singh shared with me a very important piece of information that if you eat what patients eat, you will never ever become a patient. Our body is as good as a temple. So, keep it pure and clean for the soul to reside inside it. Good nutrition creates health in all areas of our existence, all parts are interconnected. If your eyes become weak, you will have to wear spectacles. If your bones become weak, you will suffer bone diseases and fracture. If your immunity is not good, you will fall ill repeatedly. Nutrition is very important for a healthy and happy life. Body needs *different food for different organs to work efficiently.* Research tells us that plant-based diets are associated with healthier mood tastes.

The more fruits and vegetables people eat, the happier, less depressed, and more satisfied they are with their lives. Minimally processed food can lead to increased happiness and improved mental wellbeing. There are seven main nutrients that the body needs. These are carbohydrates, proteins, fats, vitamins, minerals, fiber, and water. It is important that everyone consumes these seven nutrients daily to help them build their bodies and maintain health. Nutrient rich food is low in sugar, sodium, starches, and bad fats. Improper nutrients may affect your health and mood thus impacting behavior and your outlook towards life. Lack of nutrition may affect memory and efficiency of an individual. So, eat properly, drink lots of water to work for a longer duration and stay happy. There is no harm in taking nutritional supplements as long as you take it from the prescription of doctor.

> ***"Good Nutrition will prevent 95% of all diseases."***
> **-Linus Pauling.**

Cater nutrients to every part of body to stay fit, energetic all the time and give your best in all walks of your life. Eat nutritious and stay happy and achieve more success.

❖ ❖ ❖

NATURE

"Look deep into nature, and then you will understand everything better."
-Albert Einstein

"A happy life is one which is in accordance with its own nature."
-Seneca.

The word nature normally refers to anything that is not made or caused by people; this may be mountains, plant, and animals. Adopt the pace of nature, her secret is patience. Ralph Waldo Emerson. We all must go on adventures in nature to find out where we truly belong to and learn secrets of happiness and success. Nature has a lot of benefits for us physically, mentally, and psychologically. When we get close to nature, it boosts our mood, relaxes our mind, and reduces stress and anxiety levels. Nature is VITAL for our happiness as it connects us to the outside world, gets us away from artificial light and sound, and reduces stress and anxiety.

Staying close to nature reduces anger, fear, blood pressure, heart rate, muscle tension, and production of stress hormones. Nature in human context refers to the qualities or character of a person that forms a very important part of individual's personality and is the reflection of personality to outer world which has got a close link with probability of success in life. You create friends and enemies both due to your nature; you create problems and minimize conflicts both due to nature. A person with good nature is admired both at personal level and professional front. To attain greater heights in your commercial and professional career, keep your nature such that everybody wishes to deal with you and may trust your transactions.

Let us take an example; In your family, with whom you like to share your secrets? Answer is simple. To someone whose nature is friendly and trustworthy. So, create a nature that can be considered friendly and trustworthy to attract happiness and success. Research supports that children who are better exposed to nature and natural resources showed increase level of self-esteem, are more creative and possess increased level of risk-taking appetite. *Mental health professionals suggest people to spend some time in nature to avoid many health issues and uses nature for the treatment of so many mental issues of children's like ADHD, Concentration issues and mood disorders.*

Mantra here is stay close to nature to generate a nature that attracts more happiness and success.

❖ ❖ ❖

CHAPTER 15

O OF HAPPINESS AND SUCCESS

ORIGINAL

“Root cause of unhappiness is not accepting the reality.”
-Buddha.

“Reality is created by the mind; we can change our reality by changing our mind.”
-Plato.

The moment we accept ourselves, we become beautiful. Pleasure may come from illusion but happiness can only be achieved through reality. Illusion is like a shining glass which shines if sun rays falls on it and its shine goes away with the sunset. Illusionary things and fishy things may seem beautiful and alluring for some time but in long run it’s the originality which makes you powerful, happy, and successful in life. Humans in general carry 3 faces: one what they are, one what they are showing to the outer world and one what they wish to be. The barrier to happiness is not the conflict with outside world but the internal conflicts among these semblances. We can easily fight with outside world but it is very difficult to resolve inner conflicts .Those who are happy and more successful do not MASQUERADE themselves at different places they are what they are inside and outside in this way there is a complete harmony inside out and outside in .When you are at peace with yourself, you are more open to being in present. When you are in tune with yourself, you reflect this nonverbally to others and your credibility increases manifold. Hiding and pretending can be emotionally mentally, physically, and spiritually exhausting.

Being HONEST-TO-GOODNESS allows you to breathe naturally as there is no stress and anxiety. All great businesses have been established on original ideas, all great movies are motivated by original incidents and all international brands have achieved the success by keeping transparency in their products, processes, and deliverables. Moreover, the foundation of all great relations is own unique facts and being genuine to your partners. In this way, apparentness helps in maintaining healthy and loving relationships.

Respect yourself, love yourself, *because there has never been a person like you and there never will be again.* **Originality is the certificate of credibility and authenticity which you give to yourself bringing a sense of calmness, transparency and hence attracting more happiness and success.**

OPPORTUNITIES

"In the middle of difficulty lies opportunity."
-Albert Einstein.

"Opportunities are like sunrises. If you wait too long, you miss them."
-William Arthur Ward.

God has given us life and freedom to choose how we use it. We can be indolent, self-centered or contribute to society in some form. A happy life is not the result of good fortune, action of others or resultant of some external event. It is solely the resultant of choices made by us. We all get equal opportunity in our life but if not grabbed at the right moment all goes in vain. Your happiness and success depend on how OPPORTUNISTIC you are. In other words, happiness is a choice, not an accident, not a charitable gift from the universe. It is choosing to see the adventure in every moment, choosing to understand that there will always be a light after the dark, that there is always good in every situation and every person, no matter how grim things may seem, that's the key to happiness. We always have the choice to be happy and learning attitude of happiness at times is quite frustrating but worth in the end. When we choose to be happy, things tend to work in our favor and luck also supports us.

Every threat in life brings equal number of opportunities. Whenever I come across a problem or disaster, I take it as an opportunity. Let me share with you an example: I normally don't get sick but 2 years back I was suffering from headache and strong fever which I took very lightly and continued doing my routine work but situation got worse. Later I was diagnosed with dengue as my body was not prepared to handle the threat. My fever reached dangerous life-threatening levels, but by the grace of god, strong will power and blessing of my loved ones, I recovered. This was an opportunity for me to revisit my health for 15 days and I could identify my actual well-wishers and real friends. Since then the priority of my life changed and I started giving first priority to my health and then family which was earlier used to come last. Earlier, I was giving importance to things and people which were not worth it. So, this life threat came out as an opportunity for me to take correct action. In Indian cricket the most respected person is not the one who has scored more runs but the one who has played match winning innings in otherwise almost lost matches.

> ***"There are no mistakes, only opportunities."***
> **-Tina Fey.**

Mantra here is taking every problem as an opportunity to learn or perform; the real champions are the ones who perform in odds not in even.

✣ ✣ ✣

OWNERSHIP

"Until you take ownership for your life, you will always be chasing happiness."
-Sean Stephenson.

"Claim ownership of your dreams."
-Chris Gardner.

The moment we start taking responsibility of our actions, accountability of our results and ownership of mistakes, that journey of success begins. When you own something, you take responsibility of that person or thing. Ownership is very important to ensure better performance and more success in life. There is a very good example of ownership: when you drive your newly purchased car, you get hurt even when there is a small scratch on the outer body whereas if the car belongs to your friend or relative, the same level of ownership may not exist. Similarly, couples in love marriages own the decision of their choice in contrast to arranged marriages. The difference in both situations lies in the level of ownership and commitment of their decisions.

When we own something, we take the responsibility

of all good and bad associated with it which otherwise may not be possible. Most of the time we try to blame people for our failures, may be my parents were poor they have not send me to a good school, they did not guide me, my spouse is not cooperative and supporting, the environment in our house is not good for studies, the environment in our office is not suitable for work, our country is not good for startups and so on these all statements are nothing more than excuses which keep us away from success and happiness. The biggest question is what people will say and we try to get away from our role and responsibility in the correction process.

Take ownership for the kind of life you want to live. The principle of ownership says don't try to change anyone in this world, change yourself and enjoy greater level of happiness, satisfaction, and success.

ORGANIZED

> **"For every minute spent in organizing, an hour is earned."**
> **-Benjamin Franklin.**
>
> **"Science is organized Knowledge. Wisdom is organized life."**
> **-Immanuel Kant.**

Organizing your life around your dreams and giving your best efforts, elevates the probability of success many times. If you cannot do trivial things properly, you cannot accomplish bigger goals. So be SYSTEMATIC to stay happy and achieve more success in life.

Our present state of life reflects how organized we are. If you are very busy all the time and get confused most of the time, it means you are not organized. An organized person always uses a structure and schedule to perform a task and his resources are predictable which saves lot of time that can be used to accomplish more tasks. An organized person takes the biggest advantage of law of attraction which means you attract what you want. There should be an address of everything you have, like you own a residential address for your home. One important aspect to get organized is to find your peak hour when you are most active and generate maximum efficiency. There should always be a schedule of your day rather than working in a haphazard manner.

Being in *order* can be a physical activity; organizing your home or work space or cleaning, throwing away or moving your items to another location. It can also be a mental activity by organizing your tasks and personal or professional goals to stay productive and motivated. Keeping a clean and organized home can help reduce stress and give you more LEISURE time. Being *arranged* keeps you physically as well as mentally fit and the chances of stress and depression are fewer. A messy house can cause tension among couples, families, and roommates, making you feel shame and experience embarrassment. The key to a healthier and happier life starts with making sure that your life and space is well-organized. *Really organized people are not born organized;* they must cultivate healthy habits, which then help them to stay organized. Even if you think you are a much-disorganized person, you can learn to be organized from planning things, jotting things down, stop doing irrelevant and unnecessary and doing things that matter, you will become an organized person if you're willing to learn and practice. *Best way to get organized is to write things down, make schedules and deadline, don't procrastinate, give everything a home, keep your working space clear and clean.*

An organized person is TRANQUIL and CLEAN hence no one can stop him from achieving success and staying happy.

✣ ✣ ✣

OPTIMISTIC

> **“An optimist sees an opportunity in every calamity; a pessimist sees a calamity in every opportunity.”**
> **-Winston Churchill.**
>
> **“The optimist thinks this is the best of all possible worlds. The pessimist fears it is true.”**
> **- J. Robert Oppenheimer.**

Optimism is like a magnet which attracts positivity, happiness, and success. Researchers have also found that optimists live longer. If you stay positive, good people will get attracted towards you. Optimistic people are always cheerful and they tend to see the world in a distinct way, hence are attracted to see good in everything. Optimism is a daily ritual to be followed which can generate a daily philosophy of hopefulness. Where hope exists, the heart finds happiness too. Optimistic people have healthy attitude. They live longer and experience better lifetime physical health and quicker recoveries from serious health issues.

The efficiency, productivity and confidence level of optimistic people is higher, especially during crisis. They are more courageous to take any type of risk if desired and hence increasing their success rate. They are likely to make friends quicker in social situations, and they try not to view strangers as enemies. **MK Gandhi said, "Man often becomes what he believes himself to be."** If I keep saying to myself that I cannot do a certain thing, it is possible that I may end up becoming incapable of doing it. On the contrary, if I have the belief that I can do it, I shall surely acquire the capacity to do it even if I may not have it at the beginning."

Optimism puts us in a positive orientation towards the future, which in turn affects our beliefs and behaviors. *Optimists believe that their own actions result in positive things happening and that they are responsible for their own happiness and they can expect better things to happen in the future.*

Our life is too short to be negative so always be positive, optimistic attitude will keep you happy and generate new avenues of success.

❖ ❖ ❖

CHAPTER 16

P OF HAPPINESS AND SUCCESS

PASSION

"Passion is energy. Feel the power that comes from focusing on what excites you."
-Oprah Winfrey.

"A great leader's courage to fulfill his vision comes from passion, not position."
-John C.Maxwell.

If you are not passionate about what you do, you are simply wasting your time.

Passion gives you a reason to keep learning and to work towards mastery. It can give you a reason to travel and therefore to have the new experience. So, it can be taken as one of the keys to happiness. Passion is the key to success and most of the successful people I have seen in life are passionate about their work. Passion fuels your confidence levels. Passionate person creates value for himself and others by leading the way, not showing the way. Passionate people are more confident and turn out to be great leaders. Moreover, passionate people earn the respect and confidence of other people. Passion creates excitement and excitement is something that can be shared and creates organized value, people who are excited create enthusiasm in their teams and are viewed as great leaders.

The best part about Passion is it is contagious, when you are passionate you make those around you full of beans and performance driven. Passionate people win professionals who are passionate maximize the energy of the team and are viewed as great mentors. My son is least interested in studies and he always make excuses to go to school but whenever I say go for cycling, he may even get up at 5 in the morning this is passion. If I take my example, I love taking training sessions and interacting with people since I am doing work of my passion, I never feel like working. Work may give you money but passion in work will give you respect and self-satisfaction.

All great actors, singers, sportsman, scientist, businessmen and leaders are passionate about their profession. Passion drives motivation loyalty and achievement, so follow your passion to stay happy and attract success.

❖ ❖ ❖

POSITIVE PSYCHOLOGY

"Only I can change my life. No one can do it for me."
-Carol Burnett.

"Positive thinking is the notion that if you think good thoughts, things will work out well. Optimism is the feeling of thinking things will be well and be hopeful."
-Martin Seligman.

We can achieve more happiness by cultivating a positive mental attitude and this begins by paying attention to your daily thoughts and observing them carefully throughout the day. This observation will help you identify your thinking patterns, habits, and emotional states to make corrections required if any. Positive psychology is the scientific study of the strengths and positive traits that enable individuals and communities to achieve success. Happy and unhappy people have the same pain and trauma the difference is happy people possess a disposition which helps them bounce back very quickly. When you adopt a flexible and jovial attitude, you become less dependent on external sources of validation, and trust your thoughts, emotions, and behaviors. Buoyant people are smarter and more creative, positive people have more stable and happy marriages, pragmatic people make more money, positive people are healthier and live longer, sparky people are more generous.

The traditional approach of psychology focuses on the negative aspect, that is investigating what was wrong to cure depression, trauma, and addictions. Positive psychology approach is altogether different which concentrates on strengths, achievements, capabilities, skills, peak states, and behaviors which make us more productive and happier. Positive psychology states that you have the power to take control of your happiness by choosing your thoughts, behaviors, and actions. The new age psychology works very well now -a -days in all psychological therapies and the results are also very satisfying.

***Look opportunity in every problem and accept the challenges with enthusiasm,* there will be an assertive transformation in your personality and you will get rid of many emotional barriers to attract more success and happiness.**

PROCRASTINATION

“Procrastination makes easy things hard, hard things harder.”
-Mason Cooley.

“Procrastination is the thief of time.”
-Edward Young.

According to Wikipedia, “procrastination” refers to the action of postponing a task. The real question is, Can procrastination hamper happiness? Answer is yes. The common reasons of procrastination are Low motivation, lack of interest, indecisiveness, disorganization, complexity of the task and fear of both success and failure. The famous “I don’t know” excuse – is one of the most popular excuses given when an individual is not really interested in doing a particular task. We can combat procrastination by making a disciplined effort to get to the root of the problem. Understanding what has caused procrastination in our life will give us the power to stop it.

Procrastination is the number one cause of stress.The more we put things off, the more anxious we are likely to become. Anxiety is bad for our health and bad for our relationships.By procrastinating about our finances, we can end up in serious debt. We can stop procrastination by acknowledging and accepting the responsibility, once we have accepted that we procrastinate we need to *interrogate* ourselves and make a list with all the reasons and excuses we procrastinate after it, another list is made, in which we mention what we are missing or have missed due to procrastination. Finally, we need to have a sincere and strong desire to stop procrastinating. Do keep a daily reminder saying "I will not procrastinate today, it is unproductive? Remember a powerful statement to fix your procrastination environment

Mark Twain said, "Do something every day that you don't want to do; this is the golden rule for acquiring the habit of doing your duty without pain."

Face your fear and do it anyway. Finally, if you want to stop procrastinating, get inspired and spend time with people that inspire and motivate you and get away from negative people. Identify your thinking pattern and learn to control and replace negative thinking patterns with positive ones by having a vision, purpose, and long-term goal.

***If we stop procrastinating, we feel at peace with ourselves and much happier*. Happiness is a positive emotion, and procrastination creates long term negativity, so stop procrastinating for happiness and success.**

❖ ❖ ❖

PATIENCE

“Patience is bitter, but its fruit is sweet.”
-Aristotle.

“He that can have patience can have what he will."
-Benjamin Franklin.

FORTITUDE is the key to happiness and in simple words it is the ability to accept trouble, suffering and waiting for the right time to come without getting angry or upset. Being patient allows us to be at peace with our self-thinking clearly and looking at things from different perspective. Patience is the calm acceptance that things can happen in a different order than the one you have framed in mind. Impatience can make one feel tense, physically and mentally, and it disrupts relationship with other people when they view impatient individual having bad temper and poor decision-making skills. FORBEARANCE helps solving problems in simple manner and easing and avoiding tensions if any.

Patience is commitments to the future being quite hopeful and holding the trust that things will turn out right and you wait without complaining. You visualize the end in the beginning and preserve to meet your goals. If you lack the art of patience, first you need to increase awareness in what all situations you lose patience and then practice the art of ENDURANCE don’t be in a hurry always. Some tips to increase patience don't rush to your phone the moment you start your day enjoy few moments in bed and then slowly open your eyes giving thanks to god for one more day, do meditation and pacify your breathings and finally be thankful for whatever you have. Before leaving home, ask yourself the purpose of going out and necessary preparation to complete the task for which you are going out. Let us take an example: If you are travelling to some place then reach station at least half an hour before the schedule departure to avoid hassles and unnecessary panic.

Patience increases the contentment in life and relieves you from the oceans of sufferings. **Patience when imbibed religiously brings success and happiness in life.**

PARENTS

"Every home is a university and the parents are the teacher."
-Mahatma Gandhi.

"There is no friendship, no love, like that of the parent for the children."
-Henry Ward Beecher.

Appreciate your parents you never know what sacrifices they went through for you. People look for god in search of peace, satisfaction, and prosperity but according to all the holy books, parents are the first visible God in this world. If all of us can ensure that our parents are not hurt in any manner, we will be the happiest person on this world. Keeping parents happy will also make you socially sensible, more reputed in society and the best part is that your kids will also carry the culture intact. Lord Ganesha and his brother were asked to cover the whole world;Ganesha took a round of his parents and then sat down in the feet of parents for blessing saying the world lies in the feet of my parents.

Parents are the closest well-wishers and best friends in this entire universe for kids. I have heard from most of the parents, their kids are the most valuable assets and they wish to do anything and everything for them howsoever tough it may be. In return; it is our duty and responsibility to take care of most valuable persons on earth named parents and never allow anyone to hurt them in front of your eyes. If you are a parent, keep in mind that you're each act is being recorded in the camera of your kid's eye and it is going to be played back. Parents can be happy and more successful in their professional life if kids are performing and settled in their own commitments. Happy parents mean happy kids. *Researchers have also shown that happier parents engage in more positive parental behaviors and influence positive outcomes in their children, like their child's motivation, achievement, and relationship with peers.*

Finally, if you are a kid, take care of your parents and if you are a parent, take care of your parenting style, to stay happy and successful.

CHAPTER 17

Q OF HAPPINESS AND SUCCESS

QUALIFICATION

"Education is the most powerful weapon which you can use to change the world."
-Nelson Mandela.

"In action, a great heart is the chief qualification. In work, a great head."
-Arthur Schopenhauer.

Academic Qualification is the way for ensuring success in life.

Academics are important because working people will need higher levels of education to meet the technologically demanding occupations of the future. Good qualification allows you to start your career from a good position. Qualification makes people aware about rights and opportunities available in various streams. A man with proper qualification is globally accepted as a resource for various societies and various challenges. There are lot of examples of crimes in the society against females like rape, child marriages and dowry due to lack of educational awareness and qualification.

It has been found through research that education is linked

with better living, those with more education tend to have higher incomes. Being in training field, I keep on upgrading my skill set. *Qualifications as per my understanding are not only pieces of paper rather a proof of your hard work dedication and achievement of a desired goal. Higher Qualification like MCA, Ph.D and MBBS acts as an entry pass to get into any of the developed countries.*

Mantra is acquiring recognized globally accepted qualification increases chances of a bright career and successful life ahead.

❖ ❖ ❖

QUESTION

"The man who asks a Question is a fool for a minute, the man who does not ask is a fool for life."
-Confucius.

"By doubting we are led to question, by questioning we arrive at the truth."
-Peter Abelard.

Questions are important for happiness. Ask as many questions as you can, because we are here in this world to learn and learning is a continuous process. The more questions we ask, the more information we uncover. Questions are very important in life. There are no bad answers, only bad questions. So, the more precise and clear your question is, the more precise and clear answer you are going to get. Questions play a vital role in *Stability, Harmony, Happiness and Success* in life. Most important thing is, questions have answers in them. So normally people who ask questions know the answers and when you ask question from someone, you expect an answer which you know. Example would you like to have a cup of coffee? Answer will be No and When you say you will have to have a Coffee with me today, the chances of saying no is very less in this case. You must have your lunch by this time?? Answer most probably would be **yes.**

As the names suggests, a question mark means a doubt, query, or curiosity to know something. We keep on doing things without understanding the purpose of doing it, as to why we are doing it? If before doing anything we can question our self, why I am doing this, then we can make life simpler and can generate more happiness. When we are clear about purpose of something, we keep our self-precise and focused. In this way, the chances of deviation and distraction are very less and the probability of achieving the end objective is also high. To get more success and generate more happiness out of anything or everything, asking questions is very important. This will ensure everything aligned and result oriented. When we were kids, we used to smile almost 400 times a day for small-small things and we used to get enough sleep and play time. The interesting point which I wish to bring to your kind notice is, as kids we used to ask questions often, which we stopped gradually with time as we grew up in our life. Now I think you could connect how important is asking questions for happiness and success. We are as clear in life as our questions are and I personally consider framing appropriate questions is as good as setting goals in life. The first question you should ask to yourself is, what you want out of life. This question, if answered honestly, will make your life simple and nobody can stop you from attaining success.

***In simple words, if you can precisely write your mission statement,* the chances of being successful are not less than 100% and this question will give you ample drive to work-day and night staying happy and achieving more success.**

✣ ✣ ✣

QUICK

"Be Quick but Don't Hurry."
-John Wooden.

"Be quick to learn and wise to know."
-George Burns.

To be successful you must be a good listener, quick in adapting and sensible in reacting.

Be quick in your actions, be quick in decision making, and be quick in forgiving people and forgetting bad memories. I have observed people who can quickly transit from one emotion to another and prove to be very happy, emotionally strong, and successful in long run. Have you ever noticed how many times your eyes blink in a day? It is approximately 15-20 times per minute, 1200 times per hour and 28800 times in a day. The message and something to consider here is that we need to be quick enough in life and keep on refreshing our learning, just like eyes which keep on blinking on regular basis. Eyes are the main sensory input device of body which inserts images from all around and blinking is keeping you active.

Like tiger jumps on the prey very quickly in a focused

approach, likewise we should also not squander time in over-thinking. Quickly decide and start working on your goal. Earlier you start, quicker you finish. Opportunity knocks at everyone's door; those who quickly grab the opportunity are the ones who achieve greater heights of success. Be quick enough to ask forgiveness, if you have made some mistakes. This will improve your credibility and help in correcting the mistake for future references. We all might have gone through bad experiences and bad transactions while dealing with people. *Don't keep any baggage and grudge quickly forgive the person and forget the place.*

Be quick in decision making and every aspect of your life to achieve greater happiness and *zenith* in life.

❖ ❖ ❖

QUIT

"Many of life failures are people who did not realize how close they were to success when they gave up."
-Thomas A. Edison.

"I hated every minute of training. But I said, don't quit. Suffer now and live the rest of your life as a champion!"
-Muhammad Ali.

The biggest challenge in today's technology driven world is that we have stopped actively thinking enough, before taking any decision and we prefer to be neutral. There are many situations in life where you should consider quitting for the sake of happiness and success. We all develop patterns and habits in our life with time. Some patterns are effective whereas some other not at all. Quitting patterns which are causing harm both professionally and personally are considered wise. Sometimes quitting a relation which is not working is also wise so that you can nurture a new one and ensure a peace of mind. It's okay to quit your job when your overall wellbeing is being compromised and you are not satisfied with the culture and rewards.

We all must take a stand in life for overall happiness and

the process begins from morning itself. The first thing in the morning you must quit is stop reading newspaper, in which there is a complete reservoir of negative headlines from across the world. If you really wish to read, do it later. Quit keeping a somber face as life is too short and dark. Quit keeping a corporate face at work, like we are all trained to not show real feelings at work. Having a corporate face is good for corporate, not for you. Smiling even when I am upset has always helped lift my mood and make me feel better. Quit writing huge goals. Quit eating fries and eat oranges Instead. Quit charging cell phones next to your bed. Quit inefficient multi-tasking. I realized that I can get more accomplished in less time when I am focused on one task at a time.

"Winners never quit and quitters never win."

-Vince Lombardi.

Never ever quit your purpose of life and value system for success and happiness.

✣✣✣

QUALITY

"Quality is not an act, it is a habit."
-Aristotle.

"The happiness of your life depends upon the quality of your thoughts."
-Marcus Aurelius.

You may find different people in your surroundings and what differentiates one from another are the qualities of their personalities which may be in terms of communication, looks and fitness or may be in the manner of their art of dealing with people.

To be happy and successful in life you should be sociable, expressive, enthusiastic and approachable. There can be number of sweet shops in your locality but you prefer to buy from just one.There may be number of grocery stores but you prefer to go to one.There may be a number of fruit vendors but you always prefer to go to that one.In all the above examples, all the people are selling and buying common things, which are readily available anywhere but still you prefer the one which maintains quality. The quality may be in terms of services, in terms of quality of product or in terms of post sales service which is the key differentiator.

A happy and successful person has some quality which will be the key differentiator from others.It is the quality, not the quantity of your contribution to the organization or society which makes you different.

> *It is the quality of one's convictions that determines success, not the number of followers.*
>
> **-Remus Lupin.**

Use quality words in your vocabulary, keep quality friends, maintain quality relations and always maintain quality of your work. Quality has one other definition, sometimes which says confirmation of requirement. So, align your work with the expectations of customers, peers, seniors and organization.

Maintain quality in every aspect of life to live a quality life full of happiness and success.

❖ ❖ ❖

CHAPTER 18

R OF HAPPINESS AND SUCCESS

RESPONSIBILITY

“The Price of greatness is responsibility.”
-Winston Churchill.

“If you take responsibility for yourself you will develop a hunger to accomplish your dreams.”
-Les Brown.

Being accountable is not an easy task.

It really requires courage, acceptance and a realistic view of your life’s current circumstances and one need to take personal responsibility. In order to become a responsible human being, the first desirable thing is to stop blaming and complaining. Blaming others makes you weak and complaining is getting away from responsibility. Instead of giving reactions,respond rationally keeping goals in mind and taking actions accordingly. If you really want to increase the level of responsibility, you have to increase fairness in your dealing with people and need to remain honest all the times. Take 100% responsibility of your life. Unsuccessful people blame others, whereas successful people take responsibility.

Let us take an example:If I want my daughter to score 10

CGPA in boards, then simply expecting this from my daughter will not serve any purpose.Rather giving her a platform, environment and necessary coaching to achieve the desired result is my responsibility. Keeping a check over her performance at regular intervals and extending necessary support comes under my responsibility and at the end I have to be equally accountable for the results. This way a balanced approach of expectation, accountability and results is required to ensure success. Happiness and success go away from us, the moment we expect others to do something for us and get away from our responsibility. Be responsible to yourself, your family, your friends, your job, your society, your neighbors' and ultimately to your nation. Don't think you cannot do anything.Every action matters and every small responsible effort of a responsible citizen contributes to the overall growth of the nation. Personal responsibility is not something you are born with, it builds as you practice the behaviors that make you accountable. *Personal responsibility leads to success.To achieve desired success, we have to take responsibility.*

Be responsible for whatever you do how so ever small the task may be. Your responsible attitude will attract more success and happiness.

READING

“Once you learn to read, you will be - forever free.”
-Frederick Douglass.

“Reading is to the mind what exercise is to the body.”
-Sir Richard Steele.

Reading makes you clever and books can be your best friends at all phases of life.

When times are difficult, or you are going through a painful experience a different world with ample knowledge is waiting for you that is the book world.Reading is very much similar to meditation which put our brains into a ‘pleasurable zero thinking trance’state, the same as meditation, bringing health benefits of relaxation, inner calm and creating a stress free environment. Inner calm and peace are the best source of happiness and these attributes can easily be achieved through the habit of reading. Reading helps us put our self in another's shoes; this will lead to greater understanding of world around us. Our teachers and parents always use to tell read and learn in school. We didn’t used to like the idea most of the time but now I realize they were right. Reading is, not just obligatory for high school or graduation; it will make you a better person throughout your life.

The best idea is to start you day with some positive reading to feel fresh all the day. Reading develops your imagination, improves your vocabulary, boost up your mood, helps in self-development, increases your thinking horizons, improves creativity, boosts your self-esteem and it helps you read other's mind. Let me share you an example: A lady was travelling in a train with a 7-year-old kid. They both were reading books. It was a strange situation for all of us. I asked, madam in today 's world, the kids who are born even yesterday are also playing with Smartphones and this boy is reading. How come he is not playing with phone or tablet. The woman calmly replied "Sir, kids don't listen to us they copy us."

A very small sentence but very powerful, so actually reading is important not only for us but also for kids. Reading requires discipline, dedication, and sincerity. These characteristics also improves overall personality of an individual. *I have seen MD and CEOs of many top companies carrying a self-help book during their travel which clearly indicates that reading is not only required while we are children but at all phases of life till you achieve top position in your career.*

Keep reading books of your interest to groom your personality understand people and places and achieve more success.

✤ ✤ ✤

ROLE MODEL

"To change bad habits, we must study the habits of successful role models."
-Jack Canfield.

"Role models set goals for you and try to make you as good as they are. Role models are important."
-Kasey Zacharias.

Having a role model will make your life simple and they act as constant source of inspiration. You can learn many things from role models like overcoming obstacles, learning from their mistakes, and finally becoming the best version. Positive role model influences our actions and motivates us to uncover our true potentials and overcome our loopholes. *ADULATION* is necessary for self-improvement because we have a standard that needs to be followed and help us pushing our limits. As kids, if you could recall, there is always an elder person whom we *WORSHIP* and depend for many reasons. Usually it is a parent, teacher, cousin to whom we look up and copy. Few things we do unknowingly and few things we do knowingly. They are our role models and these role models keep changing as we grow up, according to changes in our life stages. Positive role models influence our actions and motivate us to strive to *EXPLORE* our true potentials and overcome our *SHORTCOMINGS.*

All great leaders, sportsmen and high achievers have one thing in common. They all have positive role models whom they follow and end up doing better than their role models. While choosing a role model you need to be very *SELECTIVE*; one who is at top of the game, the best in their field, strong moral and a sound character. Virendra Sehwag can be a role model for cricket lovers and *SONU SOOD* can be a role model for fitness freak guys.

Norman Vincent Peale says, *"Shoot for the moon. Even if you miss, you'll land among the stars."* **This means that even if we don't attain our original goal, we are still much better than original. Role model keeps us focused and provides clarity of the path to achieve end goal.**

REWARD

"Too often, we don't give ourselves credit for the good choices we've made. Remember to give yourself credit for the things you're doing well."
-Matthew Clark.

"Happiness is the reward we get for living to the highest right we know."
-Richard Bach.

Rewards acts as a source of motivation from a kid to a man of any age. Remember the days of our childhood when we used to study on reward basis. I mean, do this you will get this, complete this, you will get this and if you score this much, you will get a bicycle or a watch. We all need motivation, so rewards keep us happy and motivated. Rewards can be in the form of cash, kind or in the form of appreciation. The grades we score in the school and college are form of rewards. The gifts we get on birthdays and festivals are form of rewards. Similarly, the increment and promotions we get in our job are also form of rewards.

It is good if we keep on getting rewards in regular

intervals. What if we don't get the expected rewards? Don't be sad as *no efforts goes in vain* you will be definitely rewarded for your efforts if not today may be some other day at this time you need to *reward yourself* in the form of *affirmative sentences and self-motivation* you may give a treat to yourself for any good thing you have done. If you set rewards for yourself, then also your work efficiency may increase many folds. *Debit and Credit cards give reward points on every transaction to the customer.* Similarly, you can also develop reward point system where in you reward yourself with some reward points based on your working and on achievement of every task you add some points and finally at the completion of desired goal, you reward yourself with a party or gift.

Keep rewarding yourself and enjoy greater happiness and attract more success.

RESPECT

"Knowledge will give you power, but character will give you respect."
-Bruce Lee.

"Respect yourself and others will respect you."
-Confucius.

Treat people the way you want yourself to be treated. Talk to people the way you want others to talk to you. Respect is not a name plate assigned to you; it is earned. Respect is all about giving and getting back. A great relationship is about two things first; find out the similarities and respect the differences. Respect and admiration may be linked to happiness because of acceptance and sense of power gained from being well respected in society, according to researchers. Respect you have earned is worth more than what is in the bank.

Respect in today's world is difficult to earn where there is a cut-throat competition. When we talk of *Veterancies* mean respect we get from others and self-respect also. People will value if you have AMOUR- PROPRE. For example: if you say the pen which I have in my pocket is the luckiest pen I ever had, as I always scored full marks whenever I write exam through this PEN. In this way, no one can underestimate the power of your pen as you have made it so important. One more example I wish to quote here is that the aura of influence and respect starts from you. The most important thing for it is self-love, which is an important element for living in present. The more you respect yourself, the more you can love yourself. Don't do compromise with your standards. Be it food, clothing, or other lifestyle values.

Accept your mistakes and forgive yourself then only you can generate more respect for yourself. Always challenge yourself that will increase your self-confidence and respect. Keeping fit and healthy will ensure greater respect from others. Speak affirmative language and keep motivating yourself.

Respect comes when you treat yourself as a unique creature of god without comparing with anyone. Respect people, places, and things you come across, to attract more happiness and success.

CHAPTER 19

S OF HAPPINESS AND SUCCESS

SELF CONTROL

"The main factor behind success is 'Self Control'."
-Rig Veda.

"If you lose self-control everything will fall."
-John Wooden.

Self-control is a great strength. You must get to a point where your mood is not dependent on the actions of someone else. Research has proved that people with higher levels of self-control are happier over both the short and long run. Higher level of self-control is correlated with educational, occupational, and social success. If we give control of our life to others, the chances of being happy and getting a great deal of success is very less. Self-control can be ensured through self-discipline which begins with mastering your thoughts. If you cannot control what you think, you cannot control what you do. ***"Self-awareness gives you the capacity to learn from your mistakes as well as your successes. It enables you to keep growing."*** **Lawrence B.**

The toughest thing in this world is self-awareness. We can talk for hours about others but whenever we get a chance to talk about ourselves, we find it difficult to speak.

So, to keep a control of self, first thing we need to know is increased self-awareness and preferred thinking patterns which you possess. Let me make it simple: People who understand and remember through pictures are termed Visual, who prefers to understand through words are termed as Verbal whereas the one who understand through emotions are termed as Kinesthetic. Now first thing you must do is know what is your preferred thinking pattern: Verbal, Visual or Kinesthetic. This will help you to learn and understand things as per your preferred thinking pattern. Secondly use this awareness to know others thinking pattern which will help you understand them in a better manner. Self-control makes you internally very strong and you may take control of your expectations from others, I mean you do your part and expect nothing that will always ensure happiness. Increased level of self-control will ensure greater extend of accountability towards the end results and enhanced self-discipline which are key desirables for success. He who controls himself, controls his life, his circumstances, and his destiny. *It is a little understood but profound truth that the man who cannot command himself under the severest external stress is unfit to guide others or to control affairs.*

It is the fundamental principle in the moral and political teachings of Confucius that before attempting to govern affairs, a man should learn to govern himself. Increase your self-control and achieve more happiness and success.

✣ ✣ ✣

SILENCE

"Silence is sometimes the best answer."
-Dalai Lama.

"Silence is a true friend who never betrays."
-Confucius.

When we are silent, we turn our thoughts and focus inwards and gain the power we need to refuel our minds. Our ego gets temporarily switched off, and we start to see the real world as it should be. When we speak our thoughts get in the way of our reality and we don't see the beauty of the world which is there around us. Silence is a time for introspection and it allows our true self to speak to our inner voice and subconscious mind. Silence is a great tool for counselors and doctors if used commercially. Silence is an extremely powerful tool both for listener as well as speaker.

A good listener attracts more friends and is socially more acceptable human being. If you want to understand the power of happiness, be the first person to get up in the morning and then observe everything around, you will have full control on the entire day. I have learnt so many things in my life through silence. It taught me that a few simple words well-spoken have more power than hours of gossips. Silence taught me to let go of distractions and focus on important things. Silence taught me what to say when and when to keep mum. Silence taught me to notice nature, take a short walk outside daily in the morning and you'll discover the wisdom and peace that nature has to offer. There is a close relation between silence and meditation. Both generates internal peace and makes you stronger from within. Daily, find some time and a place where we can understand the power of silence. Silence has really helped me in getting out of many tough times and bad phases of life. In your tough times, when things are not happening according to your desired expectations, use the power of silence and start accepting and appreciating the situations saying *"God might have some better plans for me"* and you will start looking at things from a different perspective. So, the next time you face something difficult, pause and appreciate whatever is happening. It is easy to speak but difficult to stay silent. Silence can cure anxiety if practiced regularly. You may try it the next time you feel anxious as it makes you aware of your breathing sensations. Silence has taught me prioritizing things and keeping a focused approach on goal. Silence keeps you away from conflicts and it attracts greater harmony.

"Silence is a source of great strength." **Lao Tzu.**

Silence is a powerful tool to be used wisely and it proves that effective communication can be made with fewer words and appropriate silences. ***Cherish the power of silence to attract more happiness and success, always remember Silence is golden, speech is silver.***

✣ ✣ ✣

SLEEP

"Sleep is the best medicine."
-Dalai Lama.

"Each night, when I go to sleep, I die. And the next morning, when I wake up, I am reborn."
-Mahatma Gandhi.

A sound sleep is the necessity for a healthy mind and body. During sleep our body rejuvenates, replenishes, and rebuilds and to keep our minds and bodies healthy and work with full efficiency proper rest in the form of sleep is desirable. Doctors even suggest 8 hours of sleep to humans for working efficiently. A very important thing which most of us are not aware, is that sleep is equally important for overall sense of happiness and well-being. Inadequate sleep raises human health risk in the form of heart diseases, diabetes and weakening of overall immune system. Inadequate sleep makes us dull, slow, and tired and we may suffer from poor memory. Let me give you an example: Have you ever experienced a night when a newborn baby at your house do not let you sleep? If yes, the next entire day you feel low and become impulsive to even small and little distractions.

You could now visualize how one sleepless night may take you very close to so many behavioral complications and how much impact it may have on your working, health and finally happiness. It is very simple to understand that a *WEARIED* person cannot be a happy person. Though we know our work and mood are badly impacted by extra exertion and stress, still we continue the habit which backfires badly. Improper sleep attracts negativity and mood disorders that gradually impact our happiness. People who get adequate sleep enjoy better health and happiness.

Remember sleep is of PARAMOUNT IMPORTANCE as it clears all negativity from mind, does necessary repairs, controls weight, increases energy levels and attracts positivity. **Sleep well stay happy and become more successful.**

SMILE

"Use your smile to change the world; don't let the world change your smile."
-Chinese Proverb.

"A warm smile is the universal language of kindness."
-William Arthur Ward.

Smile can be the simplest and most inexpensive way to increase beauty and to improve your looks. Be happy all the times as you may never know who may fall in love with your smile and it may act as a source of motivation for many. Let me share you an example: when you come home fatigued and exhausted from work, that one smile of your kid or spouse takes away the entire fatigue. *That* is the real power of a smile. Professionally however tough a client may be, active listening and a smile can change the entire scenario and easily solve any complicated problem. Smiling is contagious and it positively changes the way we think and feel. Smile can change the mood if you don't trust try starting your day with a smile. The genuine smile is the smile of a kid. If you really wish to inculcate smile, learn from airhostess how professionally they manage all the times dealing with variety of people and keeping a complete control of their behavior.

Smile makes you decent, composed, and courteous. The most successful people across the globe are the ones who always carry a smile on their faces. Our brain doesn't differentiate between a fake smile and original smile; Smile for brain is just a smile so keep smiling even if situation is not worth smiling. Smile has many advantages it can enlivenof your mood and keep you away from anxiety and depression. Researchers have found a strong link between good health, longevity, and smiling. Smiling makes you attractive, relieves stress boosts your immune system and the best part it increases the chances of being successful manifold. *Your smile is your logo, your personality is your business card, how you leave others feel about you may become a trademark.*

Use your smile to change the world don't let the world change your smile. **Keep smiling as it can make life simple having more fun and attracting more success.**

CHAPTER 20

T OF HAPPINESS AND SUCCESS

TRUTHFULLNESS

"Whoever is careless with the truth in small matters cannot be trusted with important matters."
-Albert Einstein.

"Happiness is when what you think, what you say, and what you do are in harmony."
-Mahatma Gandhi.

There is a strong AFFINITY between truth and happiness. The more truthful we are to our self, brighter are the chances of being happy. We can cheat anyone in this world except one, that is you yourself. People may accept any story which you tell them, but they may or may not know the original version of the story. The original version of the story is known to only one person, which is you. If Alpha the original version of the story and Beta the narrated part of story is same, then there will be a congruency in your expression and body language which requires least effort to convey or communicate anything. God always stays in the heart of truthful people as god and truth are quite synonymous. Always give attention to what your inner voice says to you, respecting that inner voice will set your soul free and you will start reaping the rewards of happiness and prosperity. True happiness comes from self-fulfillment. Self-fulfillment comes from discovering your purpose in life and fulfilling that purpose, if possible. Discovering your purpose comes through daily meditation and prayer.

Telling truth requires very less words and stories as it has only 1 version. There are two aspects of truthfulness being true to you and being true to others. Shakespeare suggested that someone who was true to themselves was unlikely to be false to others. VERACIOUS people will understand themselves and present themselves in a way they are. They always meet commitments or promises that they make. **Truthfulness is the main element of character. Brian Tracy.** Truthfulness allows you to be honest about yourself to yourself, and to others, and to live a life which reflects that.

Being truthful avoids unnecessary conflicts maintains good mental and physical health as you need not to think twice and there is a congruency inside out and outside in. **Always be truthful to yourself to attract more happiness and success.**

TECHNOLOGY

“Technology is a useful servant but a dangerous master.”
-Christian Lous Lange.

“Technology should improve your life not become your life.”
-Billy Cox.

Technology is never going to replace great trainers but technology in the hand of great trainers may do wonders. In the present era a person having edge over technology will take a lead in terms of success. But on the other hand, excessive use of technology and being a slave of technology like checking Mobile, FB, WhatsApp and Mails all the time is a big threat to happiness. If we spend most of the time in social media, we are killing our precious present moment. We all should allot specific time frames and set limits for all social platforms to increase our efficiency and avoid unnecessary distractions.

When I started writing this book there was no Corona but when I am about to finish this work, there is a pandemic named corona everywhere across the world. Earlier I was having a different opinion about the usage of technology but now due to corona, my mindset and thinking has changed for technology.

Now the only survivors in this pandemic and after this will be those who are technology driven. The success of every business depends on certain factors which include accurate analysis, research and choosing the right technology. Research has proved that those organizations that do invest in technology and choose the path of innovation increase their market share, financial figures, and overall competitiveness. In the current scenario it is proved that digital marketing is a great tool which lets you promote your product or services to the global markets while sitting in the comfort of your remote office or home.

Technology helps you in decision making and Market researchers can be done in many ways through online surveys, forums, blogs, group discussions and web. Technology allows you to maintain remote offices and growth. Customer support and satisfaction can be enhanced up to a great level through technological tools by providing a real time customer support. There are so many businesses which does not have any office or infrastructure of their own like OLA, UBER, and OYO. These brands have Crores of turnovers with virtual offices and technology support. Technology has also changed the way education is being provided using virtual platforms like ZOOM and Google meets. *Technology has changed the way banking is done these days and payments are made using apps like PAYTM and Google pay money which has no bank of their own.*

The future belongs to those who are techno-savvy and can adapt as per the latest changes. **Mantra of success here is use technology wisely to survive in the global market and stay happy.**

❖ ❖ ❖

TIME

"Your time is limited, so don't waste it living someone else's life."
-Steve Jobs.

"A man who dares to waste one hour of time has not discovered the value of life."
-Charles Darwin.

Time is actual money; an inch of time is an inch of diamond but you cannot buy that inch of time with an inch of diamond. Time management is about identifying what is important and allocating enough time each day to work on those things. *Robin Sharma says 5% of people who become hugely successful in life are the people who know, what is important and they make sure that 95% of their working hours are spent working on those important things.* The other 95% people spend their times in social media and activities that are hardly important. Time management is the most important factor that works for the success of highly successful people and it is about allocating your twenty-four hours in the right place so that you can achieve the right results. To become good at time management you need to create a plan for the day and make sure it happens. I suggest you to do the next day's planning a day before or before you go to bed.

Time is limited and we all have 24 hours in a day but the one who manages it well takes the edge, you can accomplish more with less effort. When practiced regularly it improves decision making capability, reduces stress and ensures self-discipline and growth in career. **"Time is free, but it is priceless. You can't own it, but you can use it. You can't keep it, but you can spend it. Once you have lost it you can never get it back." Harvey Mackay.**

Time management allows you to work as per your priorities rather than working according to others priority hence taking more control of life. The basic step you need to take for time management is categorize your task into important, not important, urgent, and not urgent. In this manner you can focus more on important and urgent things first then important but not urgent and delegate not important but urgent to someone else and finally either leave not important and not urgent or do it at the last. This strategy will increase probability of success. Some things which are being followed by successful people are, they start there day early, keeps everything well planned and not wasting a single minute thus ensuring maximum productivity and efficiency. Time management makes you wise enough to decide what to do and what to delegate.

Easiest way to exhibit time management is to use Pareto Principle: **First focus on 20 percent activities that are going to generate 80% of results and nobody can stop you from achieving more success and attracting more happiness.**

TRAVEL

“Cover the Earth before it covers you.”
-Dagobert D. Runes.

“Focus on the journey, not the destination. Joy is found not in finishing an activity but in doing it."
-Greg Anderson.

Traveling is real fun and excitement which increases your happiness levels before, during and after the adventure. The fun starts at the anticipation of tour itself which takes exponential growth while we do book, purchasing and even thinking of possible list of activities which we are going to do. There’s no doubt that during your travels you’re naturally excited, appreciative, less stressed, and more present. I love travelling and have traveled a lot covering entire India with top International destinations. It has increased my confidence level to a great extent and has changed my outlook and perspective towards life and people. Traveling can act as a perfect catalyst for happiness, as now I am aware of so many cultures across the world and get to know about different peoples.

Traveling has raised my self-respect as I have experienced

a lot of adventures and handled many challenging situations. In travelling, you remain excited and happy and this happiness is passed to your near and dear ones. In travelling, you gain several long-lasting memories to benefit your mental, emotional, and physical health that will ensure increase in your overall level of happiness. Frequent travelers can easily come out of their comfort zone and develops 'cope up' strategy to deal with uncertainties and challenges. These qualities are very important for success and growth. They know how to manage emotions and this self awareness increases productivity and helps people find what makes them happy in life. Traveling will help you manage fear and develop coping skills to take action despite the fear. Traveling enhances your overall knowledge, experience and makes you innovative to do things in a different manner. Traveling makes you a good negotiator and this attribute make you wise enough to identify opportunities and get the best. Negotiation skill is important in influencing others and establishing an individual as a good leader. Traveling makes you adaptable and helps you better understand differences in people and opinions.

***The best part I learned in travelling is to live in the moment, do pay any cost to travel at young age to explore the word and get the best experiences.* I remember lot of travelling experiences which bring a smile on my face. Keep travelling, explore the world around and be happier and successful.**

CHAPTER 21

U OF HAPPINESS AND SUCCESS

UNDERSTANDING

> **"Mutual understanding is the main backbone of every happy relationship."**
> **-Edmond Mbiaka**
>
> **"We are all different. Don't judge understand instead."**
> **-Roy T.Bennett**

Understanding is deeper than knowledge.

There may be many people in this world who know you but there are very few who understand you and these few are very precious for you. Understanding is paramount for success, happiness and relationship. Without understanding, you cannot make right decisions. Understanding is possible only through active listening and thinking from other person's perspective. The biggest communication problem with most of humans is that we do not listen to understand, we listen to reply. This type of communication can never be effective so replying to anyone without listening and understanding the complete situation is not going to generate desired outcome and ensure effective communication.

According to me, before reacting to any question we

have to first understand the problem in a bigger way and respond to the question with positive mindset without being judgmental. Self-awareness and understanding provides a sense of purpose and we start living life by our own values. Lack of self-awareness *DRIVE* us to live life as per others value and hence creating disappointments, panic and we end up spending our precious time and energy trying to please everyone else with little time left for ourselves to pursue what truly matters. As human being we have a natural crave to understand and to be understood and this understanding is the basic necessity of human relations. We are *accountable* for consequences of our actions and the moment we understand this truth we stop blaming others for our failures. We stop seeking external validation to prove our own worth and stop worrying about what ifs. Understanding leads to happier relationships. Understanding self and others, increases and harnesses natural health. So, for better relationship, more happiness and success understand your partner, understand your kids, understand your boss, understand your strengths, understand your limits and understand other person's situation.

This understanding of others let others also to understand you in a better way. **The attitude of understanding will help you stay happy more acceptable and more successful.**

❖ ❖ ❖

UNIVERSE

“The Universe is full of magical things patiently waiting for our wits to grow sharper.”

-Eden Phillpotts.

“To the mind that is still, the whole universe surrenders.”

-Lao Tzu.

If you really want to be happy and successful in life, then trust the COSMOS. It will bring everything you ASPIRE FOR. Sometimes you may feel down and depressed when things may not be going your way, you may think it’s not fair. That you deserve better or you may be worried, saying why this other guy has such a perfect life. Let me tell you everyone is having his or her own struggles and issues in life which we may not be aware of. Believe in yourself and universe. The day I started to trust Universe and God, I began to feel good about myself and my life. I could literally feel a warm stream flowing in me and realized that I am in safe hands. When we give our best and leave the rest for Universe, everything gets aligned perfectly. It works like magic; we start attracting people and things which are in tune with same frequency.

When we are in a bad mental state and pessimistic approach, we attract negative people. Similarly while exhibiting optimistic behavior; we attract positivity and positive people. Keep a positive and optimistic mindset, try doing things which you are scared off, to raise your self-confidence. Intuition and trust in life, work together. These are the best guides you can have to lead you in your entire life. In order to trust universe, start with little things and gradually with time, you will put your whole life in the Universe's hands. Keeping the trust that whatever is happening, is happening for good. Challenge your limits for example if you can run 5 kms try for 7 then 10 and so on. Gradually, you will be able to do more. If you're always doing the same things, you'll keep on getting the same results. So to get new, try doing something new.Keep stretching yourself and break your own records.

***Universe is full of resources, what matters is what you ask for and wish so expect nothing less than the best, maintain quality and standards in whatever you do.* Set your goals high, give your best and believe in universe to attract success and happiness.**

✣ ✣ ✣

UNINSTALL

> **"Uninstall all the apps and memories which are draining out your phone battery or brain memory".**
> **- Dr.C.K.Kantiya.**

Uninstall WhatsApp and FB for some time and feel the difference you may see in your life. Uninstalling Facebook, WhatsApp and your favorite games for some time will revive and rejuvenate your mental health. Keep doing this activity on regular basis as this will recharge your brain and help you to have a better control of your life. These social media platforms have connected people but at the same time, they have increased the number of mental health patients in a short period. I was also addicted to face book like so many other users up to last year. During those days, I used to feel anxious, depressed and like a failure by regularly comparing myself to my classmates and colleagues on FB.

There was no social media for thousands of years and now it feels like people think your life is over if you don't have it, which is ridiculous and an area of concern. There's so much negativity, fake news and show off on social media which affects our lives badly. After disabling FB, my life has shifted to a different positive note. Now I enjoy catching up with my friends, and spending lot of quality time with them. It made me realize who all are our real friends and there is a complete unexplored world outside, which we were not noticing because of the virtual social media world. I have now become more composed, balanced, confident and less anxious. This has made me a much happier person. Relinquishing Facebook was one of the best decisions I've made this year. Aside from the increased productivity that comes from not having it, I enjoy actually talking to people face to face. Do you know Smartphone users check their device after every 6.5 minutes, which works out to around 150 times a day.

Now you imagine how much humans seek happiness by external approvals. **I don't say that these apps are useless, NO but everything in control is good, make optimum use of social media and keep installing and uninstalling at regular intervals so that you don't become addict of anything.**

UPGRADE

> **"Don't downgrade your dream just to fit your reality. Upgrade your conviction to match your Destiny."**
> **-Stuart Scott**
>
> **"When you upgrade your mind your life will upgrade."**
> **-Bob Proctor.**

Upgrade and update are two requisites for happiness in the ever-changing competitive environment. Let us take a simple example: If the software of your phone is not updated, will you be able to use all its features? The answer is no. Same applies to humans if we don't upgrade our knowledge and update ourselves with the things and information that is there in the competitive market, we will not be able to survive and stand in competition with others. So, to be happy and successful, keep on updating yourself.

Let me share you some more examples: Ambassador used to be the leading car and Bajaj used to be the leading scooter in India. Where are these 2 brands now? The answer is simple, they couldn't update and upgrade with the pace of the people's expectations and demand and they become obsolete. Maruti and Hero are now generally accepted brands in their respective segments and are continuously enjoying the leadership irrespective of so many competitive brands playing in the field. Again, the answer here is they keep their fingers on the pulse as per the customer expectations. Recently Maruti has come up with a new chain of Nexa showrooms, which are selling the same Maruti engines with all advanced features of the similar segments to privilege customers in a presentable and elite manner. These brands have again not only managed to survive, but also have taken an edge over their competitors.

The mantra of success here is to adapt yourself as per the changes desired in the industry of your working and keep upgrading your knowledge and skill set to survive and become the fittest to meet Darwin’s Theory of Survival of The Fittest. Focus on upgrading your lifestyle as per the trends in society. Upgrade your gadget's, upgrade your car, upgrade your mobile, upgrade your handset, upgrade your dining spot and last but not the least upgrade the Antivirus software in your phone and laptop.

***“If you want to upgrade your circle of influence, it begins with upgrading yourself.”* Hal Elrod.**

Upgrade your Skill set and keep updating your knowledge to sustain and survive in the competitive world to attract more happiness and success.

✣ ✣ ✣

UMBERELLA

> **"Umbrella can't stop the rain but can make us to stand in rain. Confidence may not bring success but it gives power to face any challenge."**
>
> **-APJ Abdul Kalam.**
>
> **"Worrying is stupid it's like walking around with an umbrella waiting for it to rain."**
>
> **-Wiz Khalifa.**

There is one thing common in umbrella and mind. Both works when they are open. There are times in our life, when problems come like nonstop rain. Then always remember that god will always be your umbrella and soon you will get some solution. We were on a family vacation to Dalhousie in summers and my son saw an umbrella in a shop and started demanding to buy it. I said, it is not at all required in summers but he said, no I want it. Then I bought it to settle this issue. In the next 15 minutes, it started raining heavily and we four were under that umbrella, which protected us from rain. My son and I were smiling at each other and I thanked him from my heart. So, what I wish to convey is that umbrella here is a backup plan, which may be very useful for crisis. To stay happy and successful in all situations, you should have arrangements of funds and resources to take care of uncertain things in your life.

Happiness is like sharing umbrella with a stranger and feeling satisfied. In this corona pandemic crisis, the only thing which is helping people is the liquid fund, which they might have provisioned. Those who were earning and spending on daily basis and not keeping liquid fund are in a real crisis. Umbrella of success and happiness here means planning for uncertainties to handle the crisis. Bread winner of a family is like an umbrella taking care of his family all the times. If in some uncertain situation or due to demise of earning member, this umbrella is replaced by the insurance if taken, otherwise there will be a complete family crisis.

***Keep an umbrella of financial security* in the form of insurance or by covering all the liabilities so that in all the situations you can attract more happiness and consistent success at all the times.**

CHAPTER 22

V OF HAPPINESS AND SUCCESS

VISION

"Your vision will become clear only when you look into your heart. Who looks outside, dreams; who looks inside, awakens."

-Carl Jung.

"In order to carry a positive action, we must develop here a positive vision."

-Dalai Lama.

Always hold the Vision and trust the process. Visionary people normally stay happy as they have lot of innovative ideas and they can plan and anticipate in a very better way. You could see most of the big companies have their clear vision and mission statements which clearly specify what exactly they wish to do in their organization. This Vision statement keeps the organization focused and driven and whenever there is any deviation or distraction from the vision statement, corrective actions can be taken. Mission and vision are closely linked; mission statement defines what an organization is currently doing, while a vision statement is basically the goal they would like to accomplish. The mission is what people do to achieve the vision.

Well written vision and mission statement help organizational and individual aligned to the end goal. A person with proper vision in simple words is clear about the result in the beginning. Visionary people normally easily achieve their target and they are least affected by any disturbances and hurdles which come in their path of result. Being visionary ensures you that you are motivated and self-driven, which are the necessities of success and happiness. Visionary person can also anticipate the problems and challenges which they may face in future so that they can take necessary timely actions and strategies. Any person can achieve his goal through visionary approach of success. Let us take an example: A student preparing for M.B.B.S can anticipate and behave like a doctor. The moment he decides to become a doctor, this positive approach will increase the probability of his success, his subconscious mind will attract everything from universe, be it resources or people to help him achieve the goal. *The feeling of as if he is already a doctor and a clear vision statement will clear all the hurdles on the way.*

A clear vision statement will certainly ensure greater success.

VALUES

"Values are like fingerprints. Nobody's is the same, but you leave them all over everything you do."
-Elvis Presley.

"Values are the guiding principles that help you determine what is right or wrong."
-Glenn C Stewart.

Values are our highest priorities and deeply held driving forces and beliefs. Let us make it simple: Values are qualities like honesty, integrity, creativity, dedication, loyalty, courage, wisdom, and commitment. Our values are made up of everything that has happened to us in our life which includes influences from our parents, family, friends, education, religion and finally experiences. I have a question for you, what values do you live by? If you have an answer for this question, nobody can stop you from being successful. Knowing your value means knowing who you are. Most of the people are not aware about their values and that becomes the key cause of frustration and self-doubt in the journey of success, since there is no inner direction and guidance.

Our core values are what we stand for at any cost. Let us

take an example: Discipline is the value you can find in Armed Forces, so whenever I use the word discipline in my vocabulary, the first name comes in my mind is army. Passion is the value of most of the superstars as they love their work. Values serve as a practical tool for evaluation and decision-making process.

> **"When you are led by values, it doesn't cost your business, it helps your business."**
>
> **-Jerry Greenfield.**

Once defined values has an impact on every aspect of life be it behavior, decision making and relationship with others. Choose the values which are most important to you, that you believe in and that define your character, adopt these values, and live by them on daily basis. *Living your values is one of the most powerful tools available to you to help you become the person you want to be, to help you accomplish your goals and to help you lead the society.*

A value and principle-based person is mostly able to create a successful and fulfilling career. Live your values to stay happy and successful.

✣ ✣ ✣

VOICE

"Don't let the noise of other's opinions drown out your inner voice."
-Steve Jobs.

"10% of conflicts are due to difference in opinion and 90% is due to wrong tone of voice."
-Via Mariz.

The greatest gift which God has given to humans is voice. This voice and ability to communicate with everyone makes us different from other species in a significant way. Voice can be inner or outer both are equally important. Inner voice is your intuition which guides you what is wrong or right whereas outer voice is the voice through which we communicate to the outer world. Most of the problems in our life are caused by tone of the voice which means the way we use words instead of the words we use. Proper use of voice is not only important for happiness but also for success.

Effective communicators make use of their voice in a very commercial way, commercial here I mean they think before they speak. In this way, the selection and tonality of word is clear to them which reduces the chance of any conflict or unnecessary hurting of anyone's ego. Voice modulation or commercial use of voice may increase the chances of success up to a significant level. Modulation here means giving emphasis to the right word using proper pitch and speaking at a right pace so that the message gets the desired advantage. Let us take an example: Lord Krishna once was caught by his mother stealing butter and he said **"Maiya Mori me Nahi Makhan Khayo" and *later when forced to accept, he said "Maine hi Makhan khayo."*** One change in emphasis of a word has changed the entire meaning. This is effective application of voice modulation. So voice can be a wonderful asset in making you happy and increasing the probability of success.

I read somewhere that voice is the tool which connects us to our soul and it is very easy to modulate your voice to solve most of the problems and *avoid conflicts.* **Make use of your voice as an asset to live a happy life with lots of success.**

❖ ❖ ❖

VIVEKANANDA

> **"All power is within you; you can do anything and everything."**
> **- Swami Vivekananda.**
>
> **"Arise! Awake! And stop not until the goal is reached."**
> **-Swami Vivekananda.**

Swami Vivekananda, the man who impressed everyone when he opened his speech with, **"My Brothers and Sisters of America** "at the world parliament of Religion in Chicago in 1893 was an intellect and a spiritual leader. The 'National Youth Day' is celebrated as a remembrance of his birthday. The thoughts of Swami Vivekananda have changed lives of many people globally especially youth. He has been considered as one of the best inspirational motivators whose every thought is full of energy and goes deep in mind, creating an impact and positive transformation. As far as communication is considered he says, *"Talk to yourself at least once in a day otherwise you may miss meeting an excellent person in this world."* In reference to impact of thinking on your personality, he says **"Whatever you think, that you will be. If you think yourselves weak, weak you will be. If you think yourselves strong, strong you**

will be." So,keep your thinking positive and clear to become the person you really wish to be. Success formula by Swami Vivekananda is **"Take up an Idea, Make that one idea your life; dream of it; think of it; live on that idea, Let the brain, the body, muscles, nerves, every part of your body be full of that idea, and just leave every other idea alone."** This is the only tested and globally approved vaccine for success used by all globally acclaimed leaders and business tycoons.

Success cannot be expected in a day it requires continuous dedication, hard work and persistency. One needs to pass through lot of challenges and difficulties before succeeding. In reference to ideal behavior for success Swami suggests, maintain your patience and temper all the time, be courageous and honest towards all your dealings. Mantra of happiness by Swami Vivekananda is **"Let people say whatever they like, stick to your own convictions, they say."** As far as faith is concerned Swami Ji says, "Instead of doing faith and trust on others have faith in yourself first, that is the only way of satisfaction and happiness". In connection to conflicts Swami Ji says, "Whenever there is a conflict between heart and the brain, follow your heart. Heart will never betray you as the voice of heart represent voice of your intuition which acts as a laser light to help you move forward". In connections to problems, Swami Ji says, **"In a day, when you don't come across any problem-you can be sure that you are travelling in a wrong path".**

In connection to taking new challenges Swami Ji says, ***"Take risks in your Life"*** *If you win, you can lead! If you lose, you can Guide!* **We can inculcate these learnings to live a happy and successful life.**

CHAPTER 23

W OF HAPPINESS AND SUCCESS

WATCH

> **"Don't watch the clock; do what it does. Keep going."**
> **-Sam Levenson.**
>
> **"The best thing about the future is that it comes one day at a time."**
> **-Abraham Lincoln.**

It is never too late to dream, and never too early to start working on it. If you keep waiting for the right moment, it may never come at all. There are lots of things we can learn from a watch; Keep on moving, never look back and always move forward. It says that only constant thing in this universe is change. In our journey of life, we come across many people, places and experiences some good and some bad. A good experience gives us motivation to move forward whereas bad experiences and people some time put brakes in the journey of life, which acts as roadblocks for success and happiness. The greatest lessons I have learned from watch is to never look back, whatever happens until and unless the battery gets discharged. Which in human reference means if life is there, we must keep on moving. All three needles of watch; hours, minutes and seconds move with their own pace no comparisons, no competitions of size or speed with each other. This is another learning I have taken from watch; keep on competing with self and break your own records without comparing with others, as you may never know the struggle and pain of others.

Best learning from watch; set your targets short term as well as long term and be unstoppable. Opinions are like wrist watches. Everyone's watch shows a different time from the other but everyone believes that their time is accurate, so don’t get influenced by opinions of others. Rather, frame your own unbiased opinion to experience and attract the best. Watch apart from time provides an important tool. We call it alarm to wake up or set the deadlines to check your progress and take corrective actions if any. Watch alarms in other form can also be understood as challenges or problems which we come across in the journey of our lives. These alarms and challenges provide opportunities to take necessary measures and actions to attain the desired goal and expected level of success and happiness. Finally, watch has proved its utility and has become part of everybody’s life may be in the form of wristwatch, table, or wall.

You may also raise your skill set and talent in such a way that you become important for the organization and society in a way that you cannot be replaced at any cost. **Adopting these learning's of watch we can achieve more success and happiness.**

✣ ✣ ✣

WAKE UP

"Early to bed early to rise makes a man healthy, wealthy and wise".
-Benjamin Franklin.

"If you want to make your dreams come true, the first thing you have to do is wake up."
-J.M. Power.

The only way to increase the length of your day is to get up early and become a member of 5 A.M club. All business tycoons and big successful personalities of the world have a habit of getting up and starting the day early in the morning. The only way to take control of your life and day is wake up early and thank god for everything you have in this life. In the morning, everything you will find is very calm and composed. No noise, no disturbance, fresh air outside and you do what you love to do; may be a morning walk, may be exercise, may be trying your writing skills or whatever you love to do. Many of you might not have witnessed the sunrise which is a real beautiful experience witnessed by all the early risers. You get enough time to get ready, do breakfast and avoid traffic Jams in early hours. In this manner waking up early may not only increase your self-control rather it is going to increase your overall productivity and efficiency.

Getting up early reduces chances of anxiety, stress and may help getting rid of many mental health issues. Imagine a day when after a late-night party on weekend you woke up late the next day, in this manner you start day saying Oh My God!!! I got late, then you rush to do morning rituals in a hassle, which in turn increases your blood pressure, you may miss out many things in the process. You may encounter your family member may be wife or mother whatsoever is applicable to you, who come in between your priority and hence creating a complete chaos. To get rid of unnecessary chaos and conflicts, only remedy is wake up early. In this manner when you are in control of yourself, disciplined, organized naturally and the chances of being happy are more.

> ***"Work hard, stay positive and get up early. It is the best part of the day."***
> ***-George Allen.***

Continuing the habit of waking up early in long run may increase your success levels and may you achieve niche of your life.

✣ ✣ ✣

WHY

> **"The two most important days in your life are the day you are born and the day you find out why."**
> **-Mark Twain.**

> **"When you know your Why, you'll know your way."**
> **-Michael Hyatt.**

We have solved so many questions in our school and college days and proved many mathematical theorems but have you ever asked yourself why you did it? And how much beneficial they have been to you in your present career and life? How they have improved quality of your life? As the name suggests, 'why' means a doubt, question mark or curiosity to know something. We keep on doing things without understanding the purpose of doing it as why we are doing it? To attract more success and happiness today onwards, develop a habit of asking questions before doing anything. This habit of asking questions will make your life more simple, purposeful, and efficient.

When we are clear about purpose of something, we keep our self a lot more precise and focused. In this way, the chances of deviation and distraction are very less and probability of achieving the end objective is high. Why of anything and everything before doing it or taking any decision is important to decide the important and discard the less important tasks. Before taking up a task, check how it is going to contribute to my life and why it is necessary to do right now. This simple approach will change the perspective of your life and will ensure everything aligned and result oriented. Maximum numbers of why is being used by kids and you know very well how much excited they are towards leaning and how much innovative they are in completing their tasks. *Make why a daily ritual that will increase your creativity and probability of success manifold.*

The why philosophy stated here is very much inspired by the viral super hit song "Why this Kolavari Kolavari Kolavari Di" by Dhanush. **Learn more, stay curious and enjoy life full of opportunities.**

❖❖❖

WORDS

“A tongue has no bones but it’s strong enough to break a heart. Be careful in selecting words.”
-Dr.C.K.Kantiya.

“Words should be scattered like seeds, no matter how small the seed may be; if it has once found favorable ground, it unfolds its strength.”
-Seneca.

A meaningful silence is always better than meaningless word. Words are so powerful that they can make or break your career as well as relationships. In order to stay happy and be more successful in life, mastery in the usage of right words at right time is really important. We need to be polite and positive in selection of our words; it might not affect others but surely will have a great positive change in our life. The word which we use has a direct impact on our mood for example; the word ‘New’ creates curiosity, ‘Love’ creates emotions and ‘Corona’ attracts fear. Now you can very well understand that every word matters. Words have power to create perceptions which forms our beliefs, impact our behavior, and ultimately decides our life. For example, the word ‘fire’ when used in a training session creates motivation, in a theatre creates panic and in a police encounter means attack. So the same word generates different meanings and emotions depending upon context.

Words are powerful tools that we can use to uplift our personal energy and improve our lives; normally we are not conscious about the words we speak, read and expose ourselves too. Spend few minutes with a negative person and you will start feeling negative about life. Words can encourage people to achieve greatness whether words are written or spoken they have the power to break and destroy healthy environments, as well as relationships. It is vital to always speak your truth but we must be mindful about what we say and how we say it.

***Your words can change everything, so always speak from heart, use words wisely as repeated negative words may have a negative effect on your behavior.* Proper use of words will keep you happy and may create better opportunities for attracting more success.**

WORK LIFE BALANCE

> **"Never get so busy making a living that you forget to make a life."**
> **-Dolly Parton.**
>
> **"Ab to Din Raat Pe hi Aaake Rukta Hai, Mujhe Yaad hai, Pehle ek Shaam Bhi hua Karti Thi!!"**
> **-Gulzar.**

Work life balance is very important for a happy and successful life; it not only applies to working people but also to housewives. Excessive work and excessive leisure both are equally dangerous and harmful; gradually life becomes monotonous and less efficient. Work life balance is an important aspect of a healthy work environment. Maintaining work life balance helps in reducing stress and unnecessary burnouts at workplace.

Chronic stress can also negatively impact mental health because it is linked to a higher risk of depression, anxiety and insomnia. In today's competitive environment and busy world, keeping a balance between professional and personal life is not easy but very important. Researchers have also proved that a poor work life balance can result in an unhealthy level of stress, unhappiness and even reduced productivity. We can enjoy our work and personal life simultaneously by setting priorities, tracking time, concentrating on one thing at a time, respecting personal time, maintaining a healthy lifestyle, learning to say no and taking vacation on regular basis. Keep evaluating your work life balance on regular basis to take corrective actions if any. *Always remember 2 things:*

i) *Job is a temporary solution of a permanent problem.*

ii) *Don't earn so hard that you need to spend your earning back on your health at the end.*

Work life balance will allow you to perform optimally both in personal and professional life and attracting more happiness and success.

✣ ✣ ✣

CHAPTER 24

X OF HAPPINESS AND SUCCESS

X VARIABLE

"Be flexible like X which can accept any value as a variable."
-Dr.C.K.Kantiya

X is the most famous variable used in mathematics. We can learn happiness and success mantra from alphabet X. I took Maths as my key subject and one thing I remember clearly is X was my favorite variable in all the assumptions during entire mathematics .To take it on lighter note for learning purpose, the variable x never complained about the overburden by being used in all the questions. Rather this x used to feel privileged that it is actively participating and becoming part of most of the solutions of mathematical problems. The beauty of x is that it was ready to take any value and use to favor all assumptions as per your wish which means high level of flexibility and adaptability which are keys to happiness and success.

Let me share you a very interesting story which I heard in one of the training sessions: The facilitator asked participants, by taking an Empty Glass in his hand, what is the price of this glass? Participant replied 10 rupees. Now he filled the glass with milk and asked price now? Participants replied, 20 rupees. Then he asked what if it is filled with silver? Participants replied may be 50000.He again asked what if it is filled with gold, participants replied may be 50 lakhs. He then asked what if it is filled with diamond people answered may be 5 Crore. Finally, he asked what if the glass is empty participant replied 10 Rupees. Now the moral of the story is; your value is decided by what is inside you, not by what is visible to the outside world. Every one of us when we were born was just like an empty glass of this story or a variable X as discussed earlier. What we fill in this glass in the form of knowledge, talent, and domain expertise is going to decide our price, designation, and social status.

We must create our worth by constantly updating our skill set as per the demand of the competition and industry trend to stay in the race, satisfying Darwin's *Theory of Survival* of the fittest and attracting more happiness and success.

❖ ❖ ❖

XEROX

"Don't experiment on original, try experimenting Xerox".
-Dr. C. K. Kantiya

Xerox is a very popular word as far as vocabulary of students is concerned. You may recall your school and college days when we used to get lot of Xerox of Notes, Books and Worksheets. After finishing academics, Xerox of Mark sheets and CV and so on at various stages of life. One common practice we all used to follow was we used to keep our originals safe and in a different folder than Xerox for the simple reason to ensure safety. I have learned something great from the process of Xerox that can be very well applied to stay happy and achieve more success in life. Before sharing that secret, let me ask a question: Can you differentiate between photocopy and original? Yes, I can. On a lighter note, I instructed my office boy once to get some photocopies done. He did it in such a nice way that I got confused and it was difficult for me to differentiate between the two, I asked how do I differentiate them he said very innocently, the one which is warm is photocopy and the other one is original .It was really a great lesson of my life, original should always be kept safe as it is very precious but in reality what we do we take care of *Xerox that is the illusion or false things or* making false impressions to impress people.

To understand it more precisely, don't let your soul 'the original you' get affected by outside experiences and problems. If something wrong or some trouble happens in life, don't let it affect your heart and mind. Let go of it. Don't take things and people so seriously to avoid emotional imbalance. *Don't let your ego come in between your well-being, you will overcome the troubles and challenges of life if any with a smile and come up as a strong person.*

Keeping your heart and brain least affected by external turmoil's is the mantra of continuous success and happiness.

X MAS

“Christmas is a season not only of rejoicing but of reflection”.
-Winston Churchill.

“What is Christmas? It is tenderness for the past, courage for the present, hope for the future.”
-Agnes M Pharos.

X Mas is the beginning of a new year, though I am not a Christian but it is the first day of my new year preparation and next 6 days, I do a lot of activities, full of fun and excitement which includes checking and reviewing my last year resolution and actual achievements. I used to celebrate Christmas with one of my close friend C.K Abraham.

I have learnt the word celebration itself has got lot of positive vibes in it to cherish. Anybody can celebrate this pious festival by taking it as a starting point to begin planning for next year resolutions and make corrective actions if any, in the next 6 days before the beginning of actual New Year. The best thing which I like the most in Christmas is the role of Santa which is popular among all the age groups sharing gifts and spreading happiness. We can learn Success and happiness mantra from

'SANTA' which says real joy is in giving rather than taking from others. Give what you have and spread smile and positivity to create an environment of happiness and celebration. Let us become Santa in someone's life by spreading smile. It is not necessary for us to wait for Christmas in order to become Santa rather we can become any time whenever you find a person who need your help. During this Pandemic of corona, I have seen Santa's everywhere, helping needy and poor by giving food packets and ration packets. *You can also be a Santa by motivating people who are doing good work and contributing to the society in some form.*

Let us become SANTA for someone, celebrate everyday to spread happiness and achieve more success.

✣ ✣ ✣

CHAPTER 25

Y OF HAPPINESS AND SUCCESS

YESTERDAY

"Learn from Yesterday live for today and hope for tomorrow. The important thing is not to stop questioning."
-Albert Einstein.

"Yesterday is history, tomorrow is a mystery, today is a gift of God, which is why we call it the present."
-Bill Keane.

Einstein emphasizes on learning from yesterday, correcting mistakes and ensuring not to repeat them for a bright future. You may be wandering why I have used the variable yesterday in a link with happiness and success the answer is: yesterday can be used as a user manual to refer to, as and when required, so not to repeat the mistakes and patterns and also as a reference point for improvement and betterment. Do not regret your Yesterdays.By doing so, we may miss our today.

Dale Carnegie encourages everyone to live in "Day tight compartments" and it is the best advice anyone can give .According to him, in the future,half of the beds in hospitals are reserved for patients with mental health issues either because of over thinking about past and fearing too much about tomorrows.

In other words, shut off the past, shut off the future and live for today. Start living in the present, thinking everyday a new start, a new journey with lot of fun and excitement. Keep motivating yourself saying *"I am the best and today is going to be my best day."*

One major cause of unhappiness which I have found is deferring happiness. One of the elderly neighbors of mine shared an interesting insight on life. He said, that when he was in class X, his mother used to tell him, to score good marks in Boards and your life is going to settle and I will be happy. I managed to score very good scores but just after couple of days, his mother started saying, start preparing for next class, then XII. I thought life will be simple but happiness was deferred further till graduation.And then till Post Graduation,then till job, then after marriage ,then after kids, then after the kids settle down, then after retirement and so on.In the meantime, I realized and discovered that I have reached the last lap of my life. Now I regret that I have actually not lived my life, thinking too much about yesterday and planning too much about future. ***I would like to recommend everyone not to commit the mistake made by this elderly gentleman.***

Mantra here is use yesterday as reference point, live in the present and be hopeful for future.

✤ ✤ ✤

YOGA

> **“Yoga is the journey from 'me' to 'we'. Yoga makes an individual a better person in thought, action, knowledge and devotion.”**
> **-PM Narendra Modi.**
>
> **“Yoga is the journey of the self, through the self, to the self.”**
> **- The Bhagavad Gita.**

The best way to stay young forever is to make Yoga Part of your life. Yoga is not a religion; it is a science, science of well-being, science of youthfulness, and science of integrating body, mind and soul. Yogic person can take full control of his breathing which gradually changes the way you live life and look at life. Yoga increases overall flexibility energy, vitality and muscular strength that keep you active for the entire day increasing overall efficiency. It improves respiration and power of lungs to fight with all types of viral infections. It maintains a balanced metabolism which helps in increasing or decreasing weights as per the expectations. Yoga gives you a perfect body posture and protects your spine apart from maintaining healthy blood flow and pressure.

Yoga is very good for kids also as it increases the concentration and ensures a sound sleep. The best thing about yoga is it increases your self-esteem, gives you inner strength, keeps you drug free, increases self-awareness, and improves your relationships. People doing yoga are more focused, energetic, patient, healthy, self-confident, productive, and mindful. A person who does yoga develops a yogic perspective and for him what work you do is not important, how you do is more important. As per **Bhagvad Gita,** Yoga is a skill in action, to exercise yoga of action do whatever you do with full attention and devotion and you will come out with the best results. Approaching your work with your full presence and with your highest quality of attention helps you to overcome your resistance and manage distraction, it lets you do the best job you are capable of.

Yoga boosts immunity and regulates your adrenal glands and keeps you controlled and happy.

Mantra is Yoga can really transform your life making you a calm, composed, balanced, happy and better person.

✣ ✣ ✣

YELLOW

"Yellow is a color of Sunshine, Creativity, Hope, Alert and Happiness."
- Dr.C.K.Kantiya.

"Some painters transform the sun into a yellow spot; others transform a yellow spot into the sun."
-Pablo Picasso.

Colors can make us feel angry or relaxed. These reactions are rooted in psychological effects, biological conditioning, and cultural imprinting. Every color has different property and effects on our mood and behavior. Yellow is a color of sunshine, hope and happiness. Yellow can be linked to happiness, positivity, clarity, energy, optimism, enlightenment, remembrance, intellect, honor, loyalty, and joy. Color therapy is now a day's very popular wherein many psychological issues like anxiety, depression and mood disorders are treated. In this, connect people who feel dull, less excited, and unhappy are advised to be surrounded and using yellow color most of the time.

Yellow is a color of creativity and when used in traffic

lights, it says look all around then go, so when used wisely it can clearly affect happiness of an individual. When used in schools and kids' room, yellow increases the creativity of kids. I have used yellow in kid's room and have seen that it is a good reflector of light and we all know there is a direct link of brightness with positivity. *Using yellow in your life will make you more creative and positive.*

Yellow says keep looking all around before taking any step, **think innovatively and shine like sun creating more happiness and success all around.**

❖ ❖ ❖

YUVRAJ SINGH

"Fighting hard and never giving up!"
-Yuvraj Singh.

"I have failed more times than I have succeeded but never gave up and will never give up till my last breath and that's what cricket taught me."
-Yuvraj Singh.

Life of Yuvraj Singh is a perfect real time story to learn all the ups and down of life. Every Indian cricket lover is a big fan of this great player who has always played for team instead of focusing on his individual score. In his glorious journey of cricket, he has seen many highs and low, even there was a time when due to his disease, the chances of his comeback were few but his strong will power and positive attitude made it possible for him to win the battle which very few could do.

Yuvraj Singh is the only cancer survivor cricketer who has done a comeback and played again for Indian cricket team. The best things we can learn from Yuvraj is that life is full of challenges, surprises, difficulties. So be ready to handle them bravely. He is one of the few cricketers who scored perfect six sixes on all the balls of an over. Similarly, perfection is possible in any field if you are dedicated to your work and passionate about your work.

One interesting fact about Yuvraj is that he has played for the team and nation. So, I value him the most, not only as a cricketer but also as a human and a fighter to fight that battle of life against all odds.

We can learn true spirit of Happiness and Success from this legend.

❖ ❖ ❖

CHAPTER 26

Z OF HAPPINESS AND SUCCESS

ZERO

> **“In a true Zero –Defects Approach, there are no unimportant items.”**
> **-Philip Crosby.**

> **“Zero is nothing but it may change life of an individual if it is added on right side.”**
> **-Dr. C. K. Kantiya.**

Can you imagine someone celebrating Zero? I know it is difficult! But it is possible if you give positive meaning to the word ZERO. Let me share few examples. A student can celebrate ZERO Mistakes in exam. An audit can be celebrated if there are zero deviations from processes and traffic system can be awarded if there are Zero accidents in that city. Going Spiritual Zero can be defined as a state at which there are no expectations, no anxiety, no excitement, and no regrets. Zero can also be treated as a stage of meditation. We all know that zero has no value when it is on the left side of figure but it makes a huge difference when placed on the right side. It can make any big figure zero when we multiply it by zero. At times, we get distracted or disturbed by some situation. In that case, we should be flexible enough to reset our brain to zero where it can look at things neutrally and in an unbiased manner. Think of the time when there was nothing and you started as a kid and you used to get happy with small things like a toy, a small chocolate, or a hug which our parents used to give. This state is zero state of happiness and with time as we grew up, we started making life complicated by giving meaning to everything.

Zero is very important in life, in terms of its significance for happiness. Zero can be termed as a state of reset where one needs to reset and refresh thoughts to introspect and work on the gaps and deviations which have taken place and we can strategize our efforts to achieve the desired goals and desired outcome. Keep zero sessions in your daily schedule where you can think introspect and reorganize things for better results. All the Heroes started from Zero once. So, let us start our journey of happiness.

We should have zero expectations from others and bring our mind to zero state for some time through meditation to experience perfect happiness.

As far as success is concerned take ZERO distraction strategy and ZERO comprise strategy until you reach the end goal.

ZOO

"Zoo: An excellent place to study the habits of human beings."
-Evan Esar.

"Life is a Zoo in a Jungle."
-Peter De Vries.

The best way to stay young forever is to make Yoga Part of your life. Yoga is not a religion; it is a science, science of well-being, science of youthfulness, and science of integrating body, mind and soul. Yogic person can take full control of his breathing which gradually changes the way you live life and look at life. Yoga increases overall flexibility energy, vitality and muscular strength that keep you active for the entire day increasing overall efficiency. It improves respiration and power of lungs to fight with all types of viral infections. It maintains a balanced metabolism which helps in increasing or decreasing weights as per the expectations. Yoga gives you a perfect body posture and protects your spine apart from maintaining healthy blood flow and pressure.

Yoga is very good for kids also as it increases the concentration and ensures a sound sleep. The best thing about yoga is it increases your self-esteem, gives you inner strength, keeps you drug free, increases self-awareness, and improves your relationships. People doing yoga are more focused, energetic, patient, healthy, self-confident, productive, and mindful. A person who does yoga develops a yogic perspective and for him what work you do is not important, how you do is more important. As per **Bhagvad Gita,** Yoga is a skill in action, to exercise yoga of action do whatever you do with full attention and devotion and you will come out with the best results. Approaching your work with your full presence and with your highest quality of attention helps you to overcome your resistance and manage distraction, it lets you do the best job you are capable of.

Yoga boosts immunity and regulates your adrenal glands and keeps you controlled and happy.

Mantra is Yoga can really transform your life making you a calm, composed, balanced, happy and better person.

✣ ✣ ✣

ZINDAGI NA MILEGI DUBARA

“Zindagi Choti Nahi Hoti Hey,Log Jeena hi Deri se Shuru karte hai.Jab Tak Raaste Samaj Aate Hai Tab tak Lautne Ka Waqt ho Jata hai.”

-Irfan Khan.

This statement of legendary actor Irfan khan seems very apt in this pandemic situation of corona. He struggled in the early stages of his career but once he got the break, he showed his talent to everyone and got many best Actor Awards including ‘Padma Shri’.I am writing this article on the death of Irfan khan and probably the last chapter of my book which has actually justified the need and purpose of my book. Live as if you are going to die tomorrow, then only you can be the happiest and most successful person in this world. I have read and heard in many spiritual talks that human life is a reward given to us, based on our good deeds in our past life. I don’t have a proof of the same but even if we assume, it might be true.

One thing which is in our control is our present and we have to celebrate every moment of life as if it is going to be the last. I am writing this book for the last couple of years but couldn't finish for some reason or other but this corona pandemic in current scenario has resolved my excuse of having no time and being busy.There is almost no work now a days and ample time to do whatever anybody wishes to do in his life, may be singing, dancing or writing like me. Initially in the first week of this pandemic lockdown, I was very feeling low but then one day I had a deep discussion with self and decided to take this quarantine as an opportunity to finish my first book as life is very uncertain.

I am really thankful to this corona pandemic for making people realize that they were running in a race with no actual goal and they were trying to make everyone happy which was not at all desired. Rather the most important person to be taken care is you, yourself and your family.

Live every moment, celebrate every moment and attract more happiness and success as *"ZINDAGI NA MILEGI DUBARA."*

❖ ❖ ❖

CONCLUSION

In this book I have shortlisted 121 words in the A to Z format that will change the way we look at things, people and live our life. I am really happy and excited to reach at the conclusion of this book as it has been a long journey to finish the book. If I wish to summarize this book in few pointers it will be injustice to the book as every word of this book is an independent article in itself to transform your life. In order to get a quick insight and revise the learning of this book in a nutshell I am jotting down these points. Do share these happiness and success tips with your friends, relatives and colleagues for greater benefit of humanity.

Key Learning's from the book of A to Z of Happiness and Success.

✓ Accept what you cannot change, change the changeable, appreciate what you have, keep a positive attitude,use assertive mode of communication and exhibit adaptability in your behaviour to attract more happiness and success.

✓ Believe in yourself, behave the way you want others to behave, keep yourself busy and take regular breaks to stay mentally fit and attract more success.

✓ Break your comfort zone, be creative, avoid criticism, do not compare, stay calm and composed to attract happiness and success.

✓ Watch a dream, keep a diary to record the progress, eat healthy diet, imbibe discipline in your life and take right decisions to achieve your goal.

- ✓ Keep your ego in lock up, expect less, make exercise a daily routine, empathetically use emotional intelligence for better relationship more happiness and success.
- ✓ Faith in god and your capabilities will make you fearless. Make use of forget and forgive strategy to attract more happiness and success.
- ✓ Set a Goal in life, have full trust in the almighty God, always be generous and keep an attitude of gratitude without holding any grudges to attract happiness and success.
- ✓ Be a hero of your life by working hard with honesty. Stay hopeful without compromising on your health and attract more happiness and success.
- ✓ If you really want to remove insecurity from your life, follow your intuition and choose work of your interest. Maintaining integrity and being ignorant to things which are useless will attract happiness and success.
- ✓ Enjoy your job and don't be judgmental in life. Delete word jealousy from your dictionary and make use of jokes to celebrate life and communicate effectively.
- ✓ Know yourself, learn from kids, keep updating your knowledge, be kind to everyone and believe in lord Krishna's learning to attract happiness and success.
- ✓ Listen carefully, be a leader, live in the moment, love yourself, let go unnecessary things to attract more happiness and success.
- ✓ Money is not everything but is the most essential thing to accomplish most of dreams so earn well, get married to the right person, learn from mistakes, listen carefully, and meditate

regularly to attract happiness and success.

- ✓ Learn to say No, negotiate well, get away from negative people, eat nutritious and surround yourself with nature.
- ✓ Be original, fetch opportunities, get organized, take ownership, and always keep an optimistic attitude to attract happiness and success.
- ✓ Be passionate about your work, do not procrastinate, have patience for results, use positive psychological approach for solving problems and never hurt your parents to stay happy and achieve more success.
- ✓ Acquire proper qualification, keep asking questions, be quick in decision making, quit all addictions and live a quality life.
- ✓ Keep reading good literature, have a role model, reward yourself from time to time, give respect to get more respect and take hundred percent responsibility of your life.
- ✓ Take full control of your life, sleep well, maintain silence wherever desired and enjoy every moment with a smile on face.
- ✓ Be truthful to your life goals, use technology to manage time well and travel often to stay excited and happy.
- ✓ Understand people and places well, trust universe, uninstall social media apps time to time, upgrade your knowledge and keep a financial backup umbrella plan to live a happy life.
- ✓ Be vivacious, maintain your values, modulate your voice wisely and imbibe learning of Vivekananda in your life to stay happy and attract more success.
- ✓ Wake up early in the morning, keep asking why I am doing this,

maintain a work life balance, use words commercially and keep on moving forward like a watch to achieve your goal.

✓ Be flexible like variable X,do regular X ray of your actions and celebrate life by being the SANTA of someone's life.

✓ Make Yoga an integral part of your life, use Yesterday as a reference point and get motivation from Yuvraj to handle challenges of life and attract more success.

✓ Observe animals in zoo to better understand human habits, keep adding zeros to your income, live life king size enjoying every moment as if you are going to die tomorrow as **"ZINDAGI NA MILEGI DUBARA".**

ACKNOWLEDGEMENTS

I am really JUBILANT to share that I have finally completed this book. This would not have been possible without the support of many people who have AIDED me personally and professionally.Primarily, I am grateful to acknowledge the support and cooperation of my wife **Shanta** and my father **Capt. Hanuman Kantiya** for motivating me to contribute something to the society in the form of writing. I appreciate my daughter **NUPUR** and son **ARNAV** who supported my spirits with their SOLICITUDES and smiles.

*Big thanks to **Mrs. Neha Sharma**, Pranali , Miral and Sachin from Editorial team for proof reading and making the language of book more legible. Special Thanks to **Col.Pracheesh Tiwari** for the concept,RJ Rex for PR support, Rajiv for technical support* and Preeti Parashar(Author of Best Selling book"**@The click of love**") for inspiration.

I wish to mention the blessings of my mentors whose guidance and teachings have helped me; namely Dr.C.R.Choudhary, Dr.Priydashi Patni, Dr.Ashwini Sharma, Dr.Ravi Ghuntey, Dr.Haridas Vyas, Dr.L.N Bunkar, Dr.Abha Purohit, Dr.Arpita Kakkar, Dr.Gaurav Lodha, Dr.Mahendra Kumar, Mukul Goswami Sir, Ravi Mohata Sir, Mukesh Bansal Sir, Mahendra Lalas Sir, Zafar Sir, S.L.Chowdhary Sir, Raman Sir, Sandeep Sir, Zakir Sir, Shri R.K Raina Sir, Shri Aseem Mishra Sir, Pankaja Sir, Varun Sir, Saurabh Sir, Zubair Sir, Yogesh Chandak Sir, Himanshu Arora Sir and Magan Kalra Sir.

Last and certainly not the least: Thank you my school friends, college friends and Generator of Diversity, **Lord Shiva**.

NOTES

NOTES